Origami Worldwide

Other books by John Montroll:

Dinosaur Origami

Mythological Creatures and the Chinese Zodiac Origami

Teach Yourself Origami

Origami Under the Sea by John Montroll and Robert J. Lang

Sea Creatures in Origami by John Montroll and Robert J. Lang

Bringing Origami to Life

Bugs and Birds in Origami

Dollar Bill Animals in Origami

Dollar Bill Origami

Easy Dollar Bill Origami

Super Simple Origami

A Constellation of Origami Polyhedra

Classic Polyhedra Origami

Storytime Origami

Christmas Origami

Easy Christmas Origami

Animal Origami for the Enthusiast

Origami for the Enthusiast

Easy Origami

Birds in Origami

Favorite Animals in Origami

Origami Worldwide

John Montroll and Brian K. Webb

Dover Publications, Inc.
New York

To Erica, Kira, Selena, and Jana

Copyright

Library of Congress Cataloging-in-Publication Data

Origami worldwide / edited by John Montroll and Brian K. Webb.
p. cm.
ISBN 978-0-486-48362-7
1. Origami. I. Montroll, John. II. Webb, Brian K.
TT870.O63 2011   ISBN-10: 0-486-48362-2   2011
736'.982–dc22
2011011343

Manufactured in the United States
48362201
www.doverpublications.com

Introduction

rigami Worldwide is a collection of models created by some of the most exciting origami designers, that we have traveled the world to find. These models were collected over the past several years from folders that we had the good fortune to meet at national conventions, local group meetings, and over the internet. You will find that many countries are represented here from around the world, including: Australia, Bolivia, Chile, China, Canada, France, Hungary, India, Italy, Japan, South Africa, Switzerland, The Netherlands, United Kingdom, Uruguay, USA, and Vietnam.

In Origami Worldwide, you will find an impressive collection of origami models of varying difficulty to fold. Designers with various styles and subjects are represented. Some of the easier models are Penguin from France, Boat from India, and Frogs from England and Uruguay. Some of the unusual intermediate models are Ganesha from India, Ocean Liner from England, and Solicino (pretty Sun) from Italy. On the more complex side are the detailed Snail from Holland, Fiery Dragon from China, and Eric Joisel's Cat from France.

The diagrams are drawn in the internationally approved Randlett-Yoshizawa style, which is easy to follow once you have learned the basic folds. You can use any kind of square paper for these models, but the best results can be achieved using standard origami paper, which is colored on one side and white on the other. In these diagrams, the shading represents the colored side. Large sheets are easier to use than small ones. Origami supplies can be found in arts and craft shops, or visit Dover Publications online at www.doverpublications.com, or OrigamiUSA at www.origami-usa.org. You can find local and national groups practicing the art of origami around the world with online sites like Origami USA's .

We want to thank all the origami designers that contributed models: Nick Robinson, Mark Bolitho, Nicolas Terry, Eric Joisel, Peter Budai, Sipho Mabona, Federico Scalambra, Nicoletta Maggino, Ryan Walsh, Helen Lee, John Szinger, Robert J. Lang, Miguel A. Callisaya, Patricio Kunz Tomic, Roman Diaz, Gareth Louis, Steven Casey, Quentin Trollip, Kuldip Thatte, Kamlesh Gandi, Fumiaki Kawahata, Nguyen Hung Cuong, and Kade Chan Pak Hei. I also give thanks to Himanshu Agrawal for folding the models for the cover. We couldn't have done it without your kindness and patience.

It is our plan that folding these models will spark a lifelong interest in this ancient art form that will then spawn new friendships for you that can span the globe and a lifetime, as it has for us.

John Montroll
Brian K. Webb

www.johnmontroll.com

Contents

★   Simple
★★   Intermediate
★★★ Complex

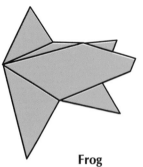

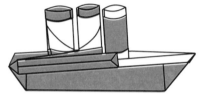

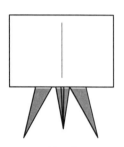

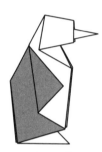

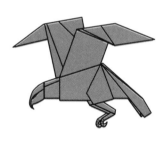

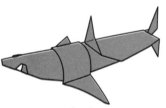

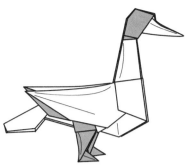

Gannet
Ryan Welsh, The Netherlands
★★
page 44

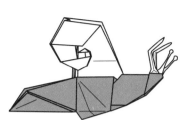

Snail
Ryan Welsh, The Netherlands
★★★
page 48

Heart in Heart
Helen Lee, Canada
★★
page 54

Diver Down Flag
Brian K. Webb, USA
★★
page 57

Santa
Brian K. Webb, USA
★★
page 59

Rhinoceros
John Montroll, USA
★★
page 62

Hot Air Balloon
John Szinger, USA
★★
page 65

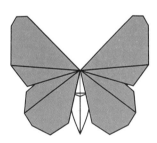

Tropical Morpho Butterfly
Robert J. Lang, USA
★★★
page 69

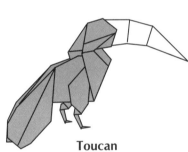

Toucan
Miguel A. Callisaya, Bolivia
★★
page 73

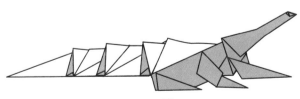

Crocodile
Patricio Kunz Tomic, Chile
★★★
page 76

Smiling Frog
Roman Diaz, Uruguay
★★
page 81

more →

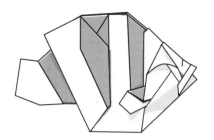

Reef Fish
Roman Diaz, Uruguay
★★★
page 83

Rooster
Gareth Louis, Australia
★★
page 86

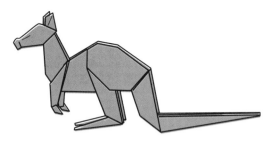

Kangaroo
Steven Casey, Australia
★★★
page 89

Cocounut Tree
Quentin Trollip, South Africa
★★★
page 93

Polar Bear
Quentin Trollip, South Africa
★★★
page 98

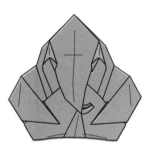

Ganesha
Kamlesh Gandhi, India
★★
page 104

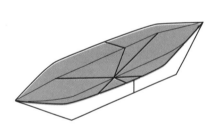

Boat
Kuldip Thatte, India
★
page 107

Fox
Fumiaki Kawahata, Japan
★★
page 108

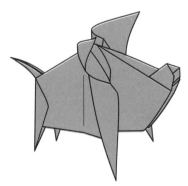

Pig
Nguyen Hung Cuong, Vietnam
★★
page 110

Fiery Dragon
Kade Chan Pak Hei, China
★★★
page 113

Symbols

Lines

— — — — — — — — —   Valley fold, fold in front.

—·—·—·—·—·—·—   Mountain fold, fold behind.

_____   Crease line.

....   X-ray or guide line.

Arrows

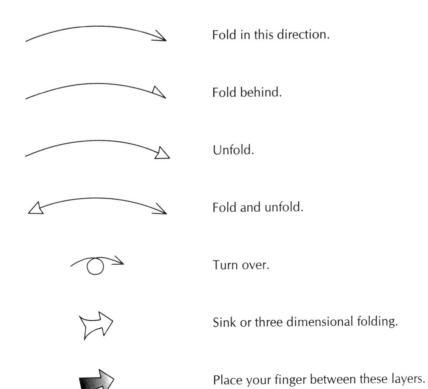

Fold in this direction.

Fold behind.

Unfold.

Fold and unfold.

Turn over.

Sink or three dimensional folding.

Place your finger between these layers.

Ali's Dish #2

Designed by Nick Robinson
United Kingdom

Originally diagrammed by
Nick Robinson

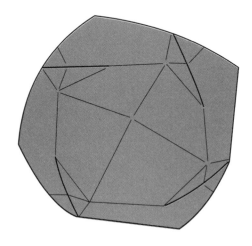

Nick is a British origami professional who specializes in the simpler end of the origami spectrum. His website is www.origami.me.uk. Ali's dish is named after his wife, an origami widow for many years.

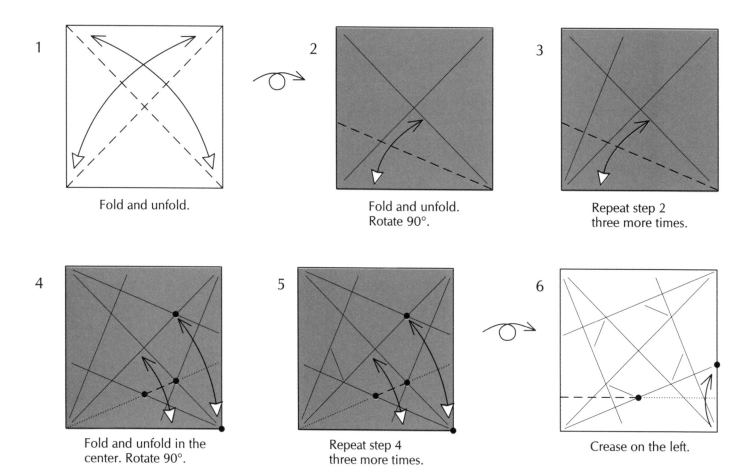

1 Fold and unfold.

2 Fold and unfold.
Rotate 90°.

3 Repeat step 2
three more times.

4 Fold and unfold in the
center. Rotate 90°.

5 Repeat step 4
three more times.

6 Crease on the left.

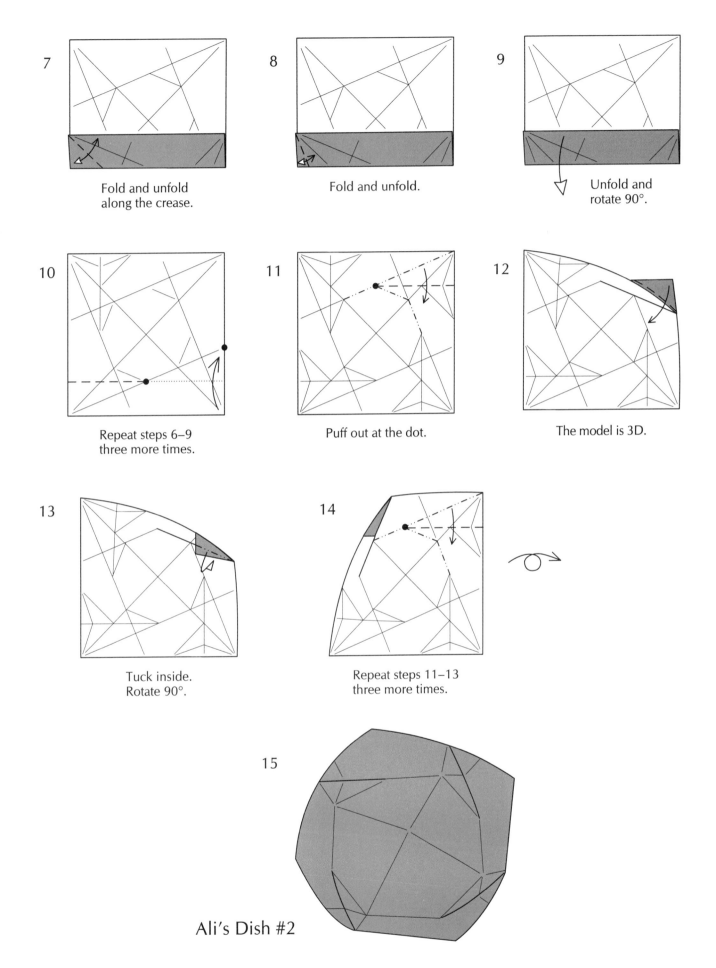

7

Fold and unfold
along the crease.

8

Fold and unfold.

9

Unfold and
rotate 90°.

10

Repeat steps 6–9
three more times.

11

Puff out at the dot.

12

The model is 3D.

13

Tuck inside.
Rotate 90°.

14

Repeat steps 11–13
three more times.

15

Ali's Dish #2

Frog

Designed by Nick Robinson
United Kingdom

Originally diagrammed by
Nick Robinson

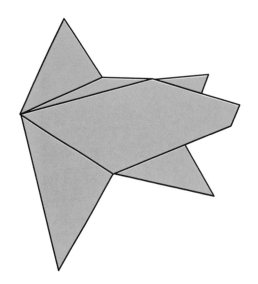

1

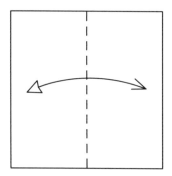

Fold and unfold.

2

Fold and unfold.

3

1. Fold and unfold.
2. Fold down

4

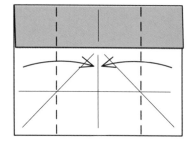

Fold to the center.

5

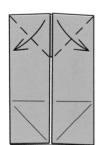

6

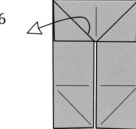

Pull out the
hidden corner.

7

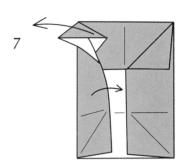

A 3D intermediate step. Repeat steps 6–7 on the right.

8

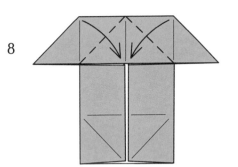

9

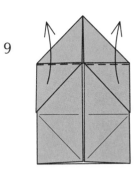

10

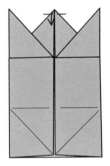

Fold the tip down.

11

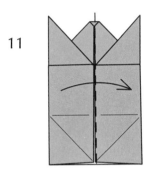

Fold in half.

12

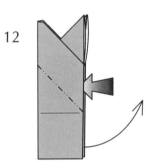

Reverse-fold.

13

A 3D intermediate step.

14

Squash-fold. Repeat behind.

15

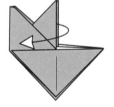

Spread.

16

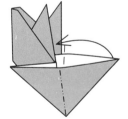

This is an asymmetric reverse fold. Fold inside.

17

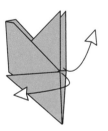

Spread.

18

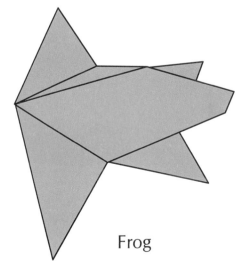

Frog

Ocean Liner

Designed by Mark Bolitho
England

Originally diagrammed by
Mark Bolitho

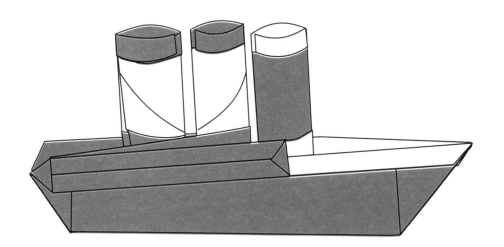

Mark Bolitho is one of the United Kingdom's most established origami designers. He has been involved with paper folding since childhood. In 2004 he started working full time as an origami designer through his website www.creaselightning.co.uk. In 2006 he was elected General Secretary of the British Origami Society and continues to support its work. The British Origami Society (www.britishorigami.info) is one of the oldest origami societies in the world. Established in 1967, it has been a foundation of support to origami enthusiasts in both the United Kingdom and the members it attracts around the world.

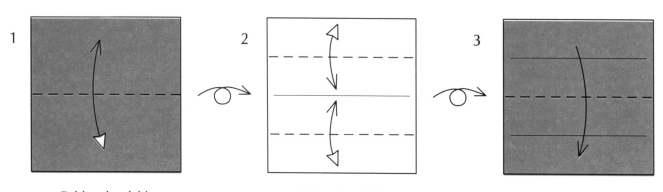

1 Fold and unfold.

2 Fold and unfold.

3

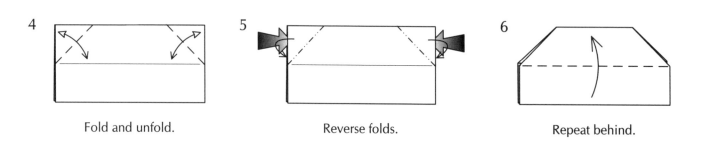

4 Fold and unfold.

5 Reverse folds.

6 Repeat behind.

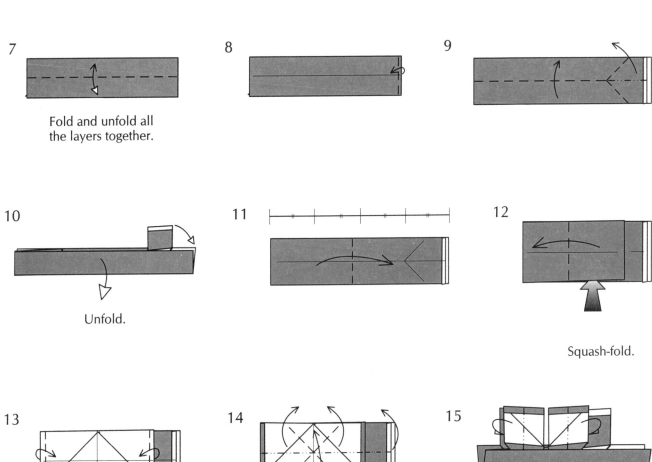

7

Fold and unfold all
the layers together.

8

9

10

Unfold.

11

12

Squash-fold.

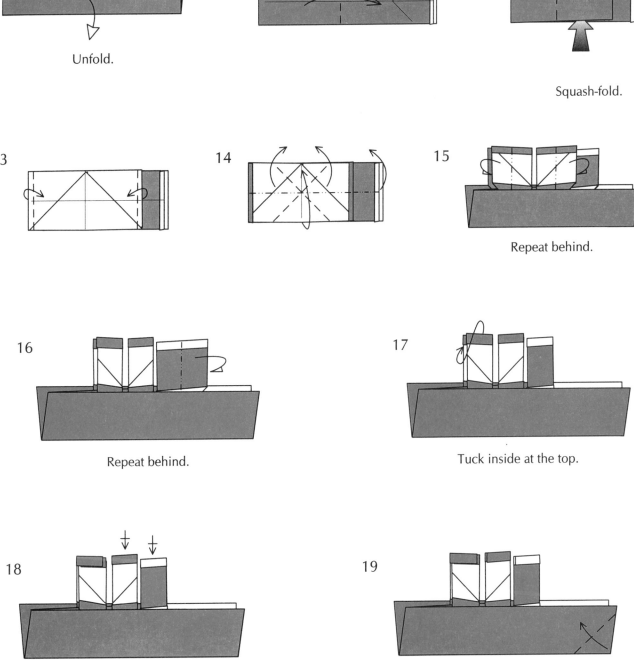

13

14

15

Repeat behind.

16

Repeat behind.

17

Tuck inside at the top.

18

Repeat step 17 two more times.

19

20

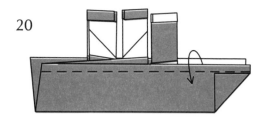

Repeat behind.

21

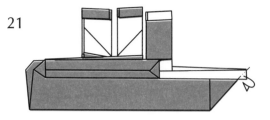

Repeat behind.

22

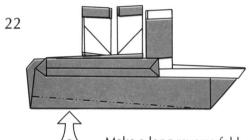

Make a long reverse fold.

23

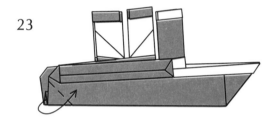

Repeat behind.

24

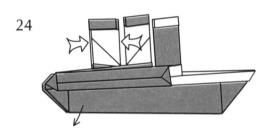

Curl the smoke stack. Repeat for the
other two. Spread at the bottom.

25

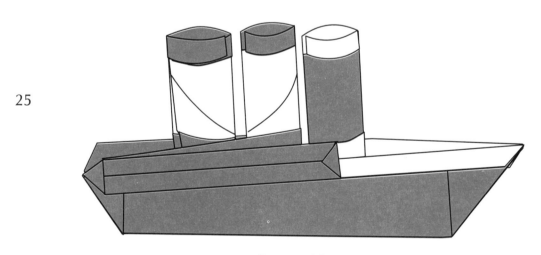

Ocean Liner

Easel

Designed by Mark Bolitho
England

Originally diagrammed by
Mark Bolitho

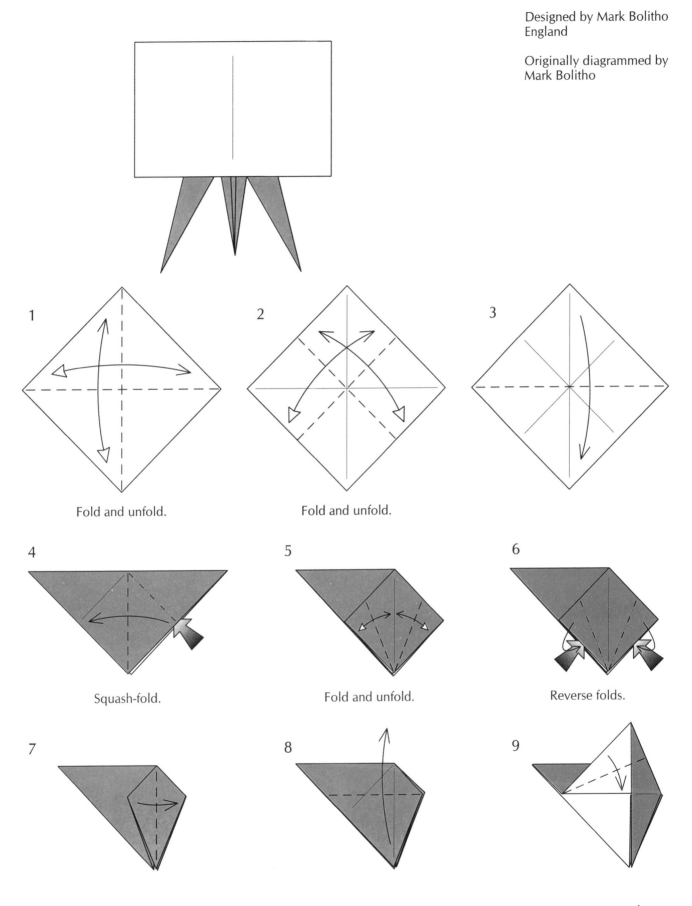

1 Fold and unfold.

2 Fold and unfold.

3

4 Squash-fold.

5 Fold and unfold.

6 Reverse folds.

7

8

9

10

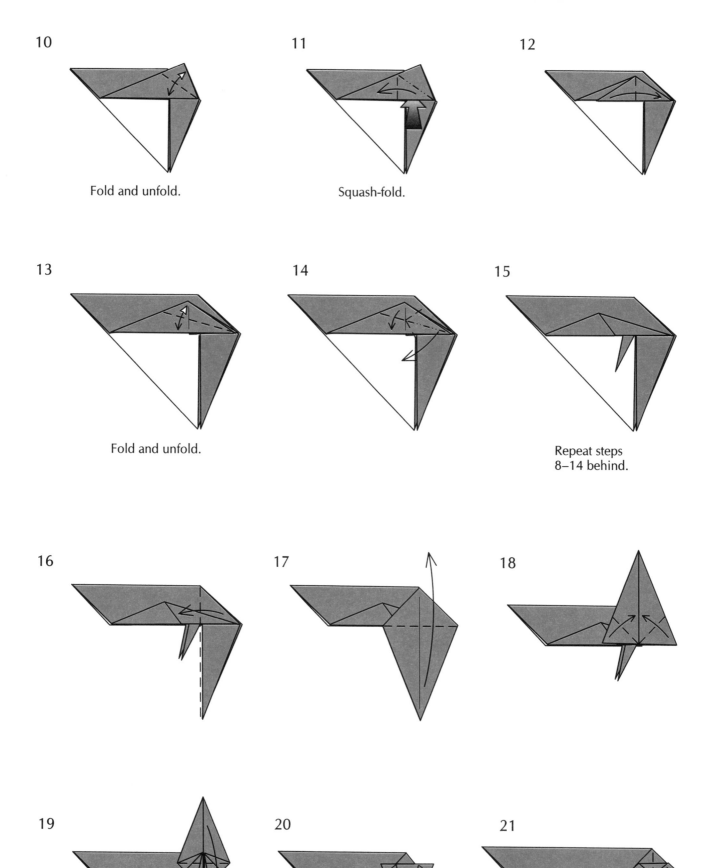

Fold and unfold.

11

Squash-fold.

12

13

Fold and unfold.

14

15

Repeat steps
8–14 behind.

16

17

18

19

20

21

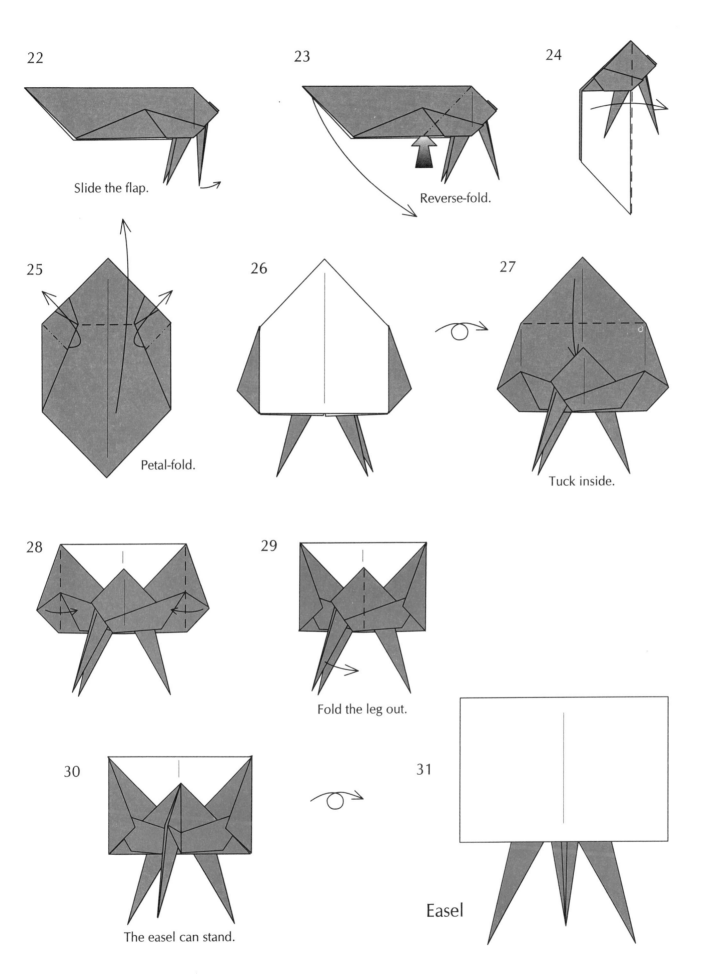

22

Slide the flap.

23

Reverse-fold.

24

25

Petal-fold.

26

27

Tuck inside.

28

29

Fold the leg out.

30

The easel can stand.

31

Easel

Penguin

Designed by Nicolas Terry
France

Originally diagrammed by
Nicolas Terry

Please visit Nicolas Terry's
website at passionorigami.com

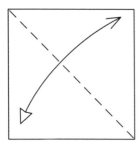

1

Fold and unfold.

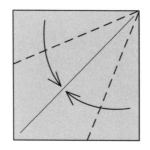

2

Valley-fold to kite base.

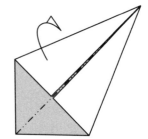

3

Mountain-fold in half.

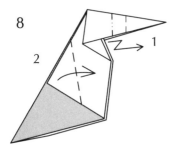

4

Fold and unfold.

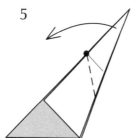

5

Fold the layers
together.

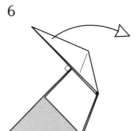

6

Note the right
angle. Unfold.

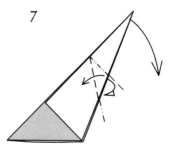

7

Fold along the creases
for this crimp fold.

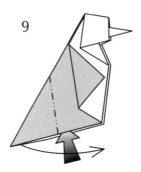

8

1. Crimp-fold the beak.
2. Repeat behind.
There are no landmarks
for these folds.

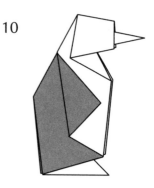

9

Reverse-fold.

10

Penguin

Eagle

Designed by Nicolas Terry
France

Originally diagrammed by
Nicolas Terry

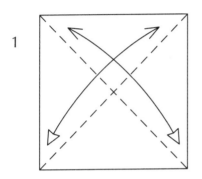

1

Fold and unfold.

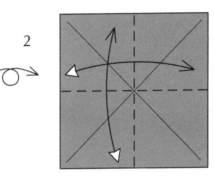

2

Fold and unfold.

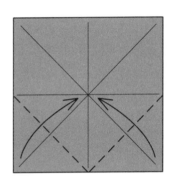

3

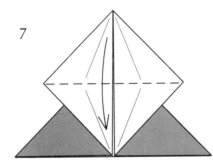

4

Fold along the creases.

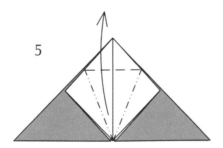

5

Petal-fold.

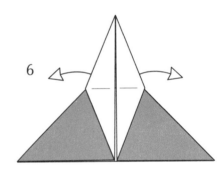

6

Unlock and pull out
the hidden corners.

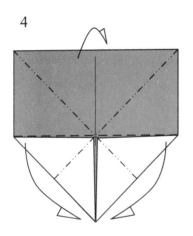

7

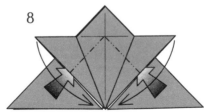

8

Reverse folds.

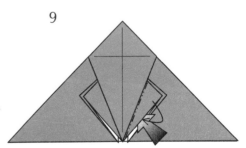

9

Reverse-fold.

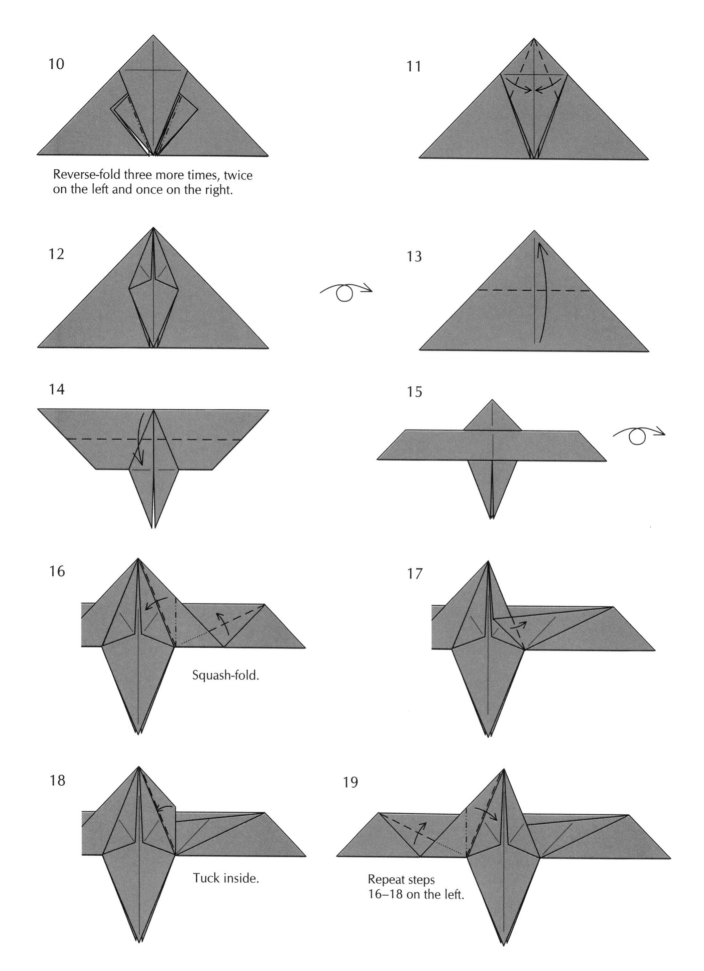

10

Reverse-fold three more times, twice on the left and once on the right.

11

12

13

14

15

16

Squash-fold.

17

18

Tuck inside.

19

Repeat steps 16–18 on the left.

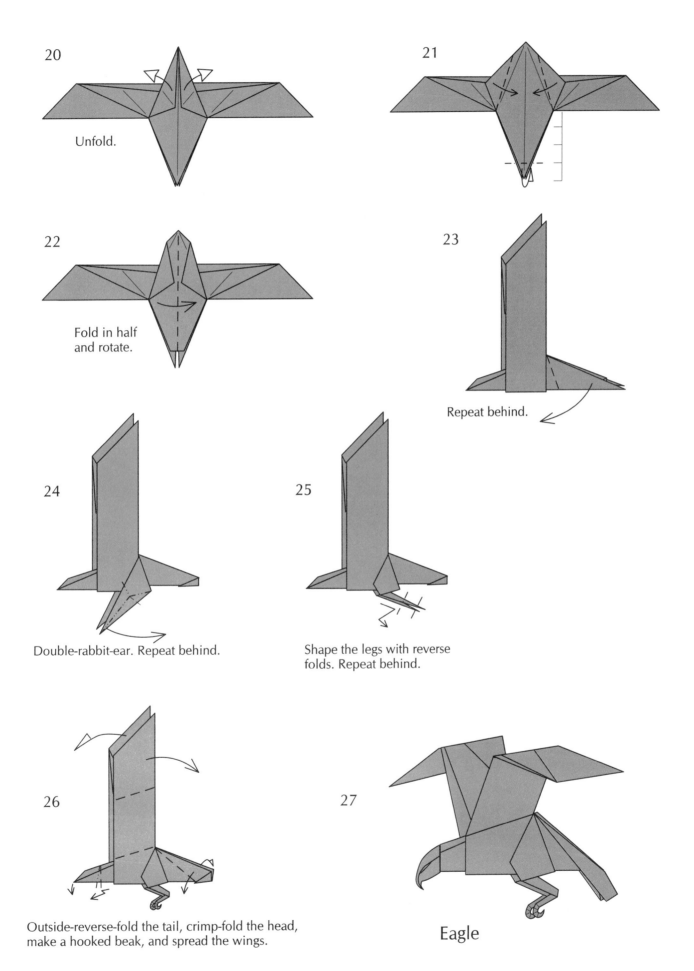

20

Unfold.

21

22

Fold in half
and rotate.

23

Repeat behind.

24

Double-rabbit-ear. Repeat behind.

25

Shape the legs with reverse
folds. Repeat behind.

26

Outside-reverse-fold the tail, crimp-fold the head,
make a hooked beak, and spread the wings.

27

Eagle

Shark

Designed by Nicolas Terry
France

Originally diagrammed by
Nicolas Terry

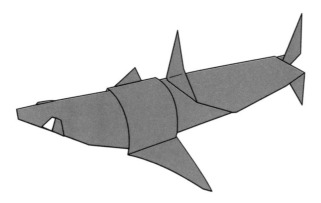

1

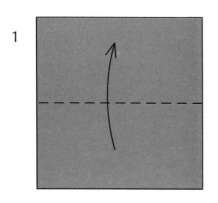

2

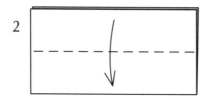

Repeat behind.

3

Fold and unfold.
Repeat behind.

4

Fold and unfold.
Repeat behind.

5

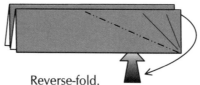

Reverse-fold.

6

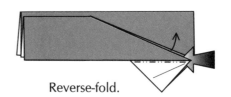

Reverse-fold.

7

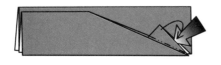

Reverse-fold.

8

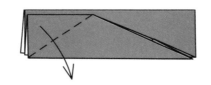

9

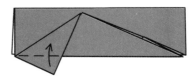

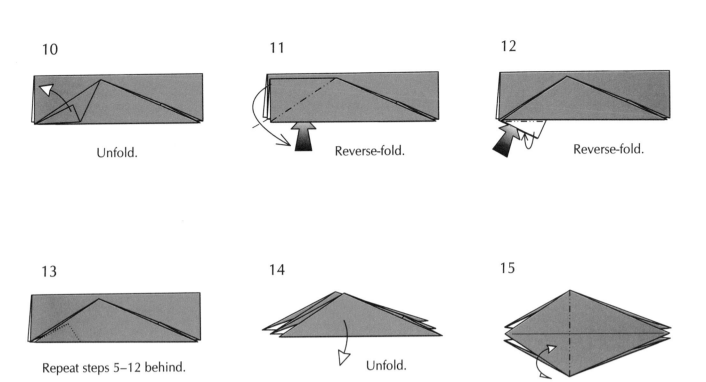

10

Unfold.

11

Reverse-fold.

12

Reverse-fold.

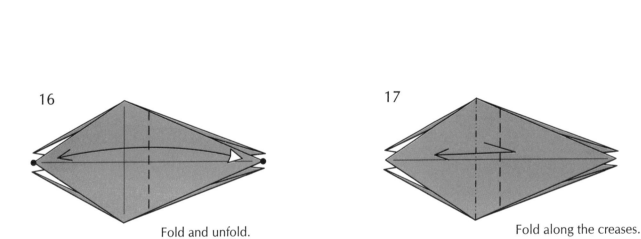

13

Repeat steps 5–12 behind.

14

Unfold.

15

Fold and unfold.

16

Fold and unfold.

17

Fold along the creases.

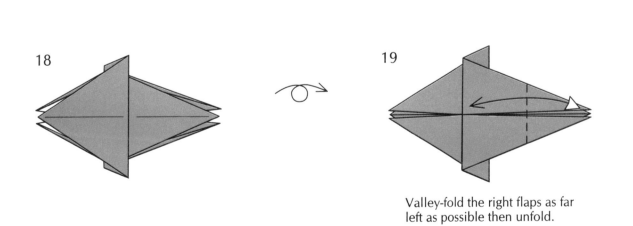

18

19

Valley-fold the right flaps as far
left as possible then unfold.

20

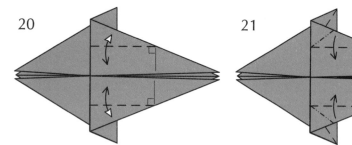

Crease the top layer.

21

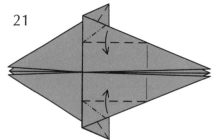

Squash folds.

22

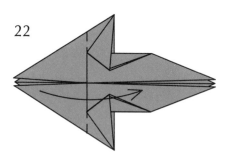

23

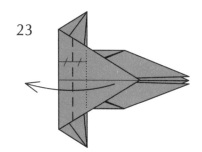

24

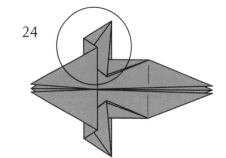

The fin will be enlarged.

25

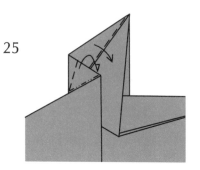

26

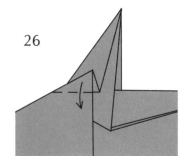

27

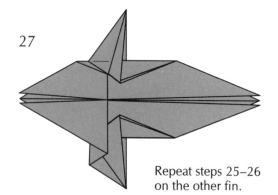

Repeat steps 25–26
on the other fin.

28

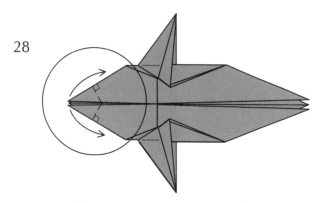

There are no guides. The bigger the
flaps are, the larger the eyes will be.

29

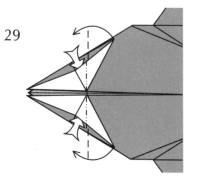

Squash folds.

30

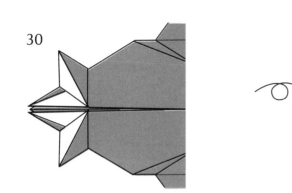

31

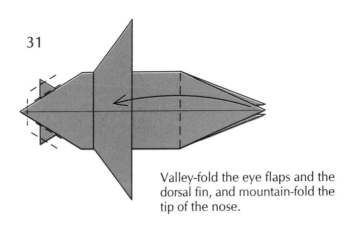

Valley-fold the eye flaps and the dorsal fin, and mountain-fold the tip of the nose.

32

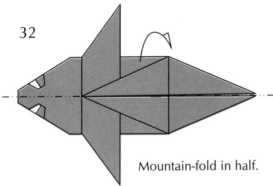

Mountain-fold in half.

33

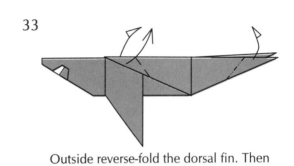

Outside reverse-fold the dorsal fin. Then mountain-fold the top flap of the tail.

34

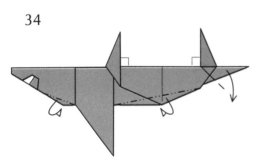

Note the right angles by the fin and tail. Mountain-fold the body and repeat behind. Then valley-fold the second tail flap.

35

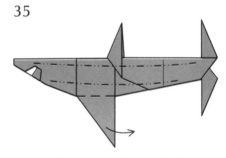

Round the body. Repeat behind.

36

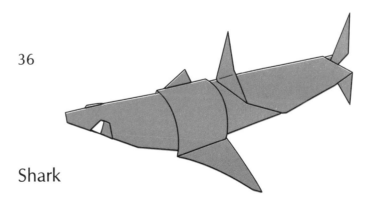

Shark

Cat

Designed by Eric Joisel
France

Originally diagrammed by
Eric Joisel

The diagrams are not intended to be precise. It
is up to you to produce your own variations.

Website: http://www.ericjoisel.com/

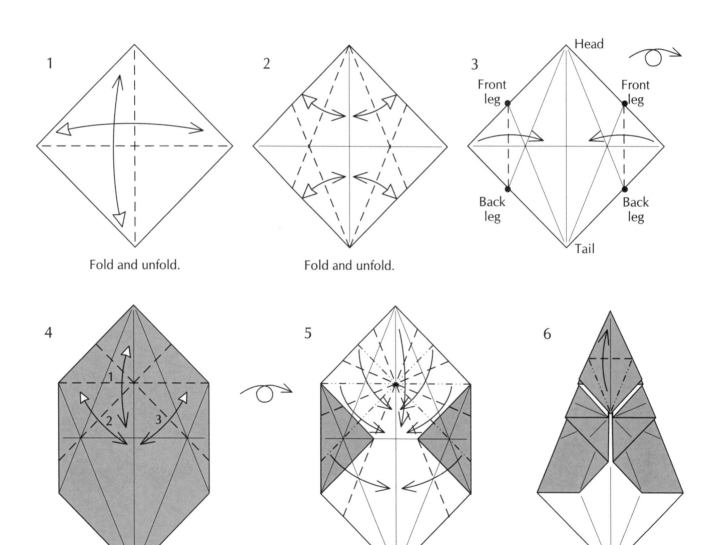

1 Fold and unfold.

2 Fold and unfold.

3 Head / Front leg / Front leg / Back leg / Back leg / Tail

4 Fold and unfold in
the order shown.

5 Collapse along the creases.

6 Petal-fold.

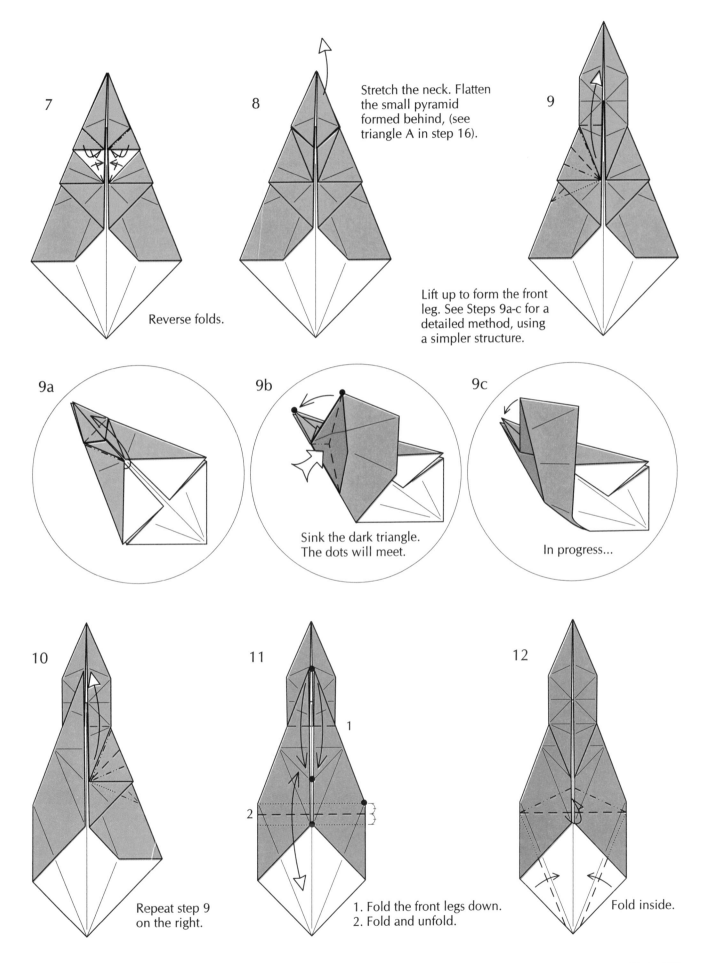

7

Reverse folds.

8

Stretch the neck. Flatten the small pyramid formed behind, (see triangle A in step 16).

9

Lift up to form the front leg. See Steps 9a-c for a detailed method, using a simpler structure.

9a

9b

Sink the dark triangle. The dots will meet.

9c

In progress...

10

Repeat step 9 on the right.

11

1. Fold the front legs down.
2. Fold and unfold.

12

Fold inside.

Cat 29

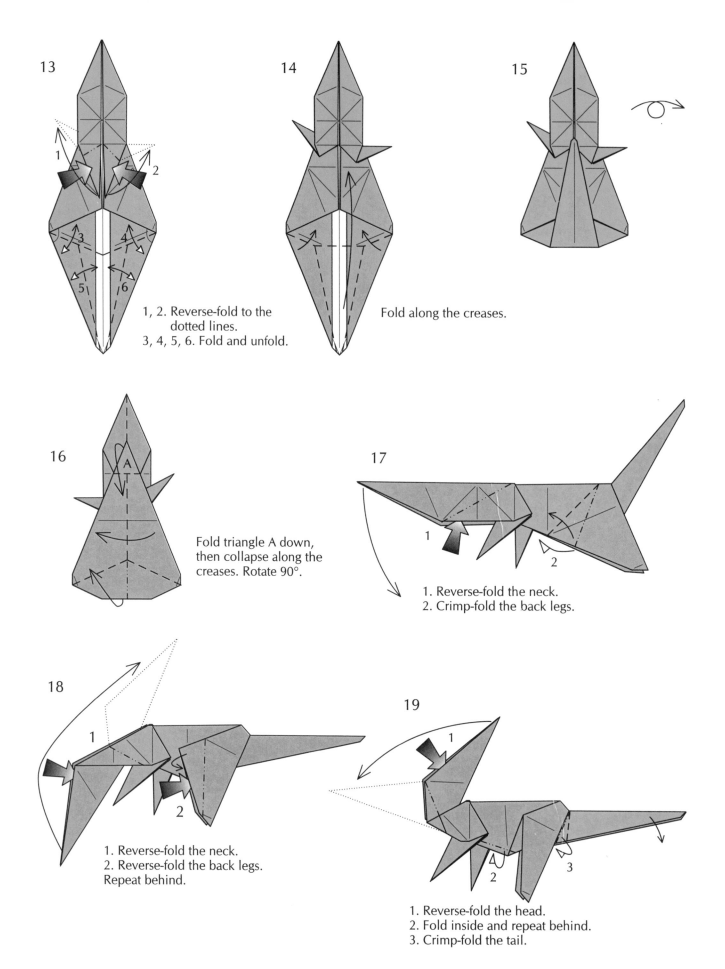

13

1, 2. Reverse-fold to the dotted lines.
3, 4, 5, 6. Fold and unfold.

14

Fold along the creases.

15

16

Fold triangle A down, then collapse along the creases. Rotate 90°.

17

1. Reverse-fold the neck.
2. Crimp-fold the back legs.

18

1. Reverse-fold the neck.
2. Reverse-fold the back legs. Repeat behind.

19

1. Reverse-fold the head.
2. Fold inside and repeat behind.
3. Crimp-fold the tail.

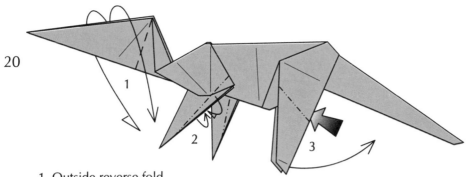

20

1. Outside-reverse-fold.
2. Thin the front legs.
3. Reverse-fold the back legs.
Repeat behind.

21

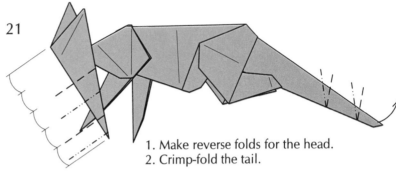

1. Make reverse folds for the head.
2. Crimp-fold the tail.

22

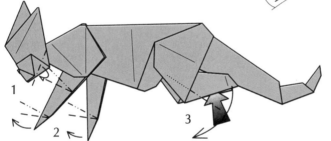

1. Fold behind on the head.
2. Crimp-fold the front legs.
3. Reverse-fold the back legs.
Repeat behind.

23

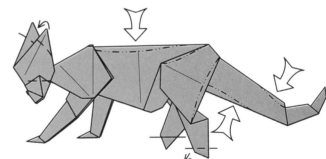

Outside-reverse-fold the ears, open the
eyes, shape the back, release the loose
paper at the back feet. Repeat behind.

24

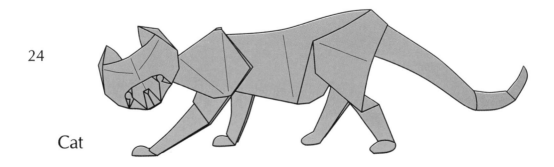

Cat

Mr. Moustache

Designed by Peter Budai
Hungary

Originally diagrammed by
Peter Budai

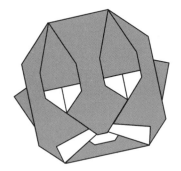

Visit Peter Budai's website at
http://www.budaiorigami.hu

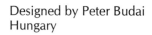

1

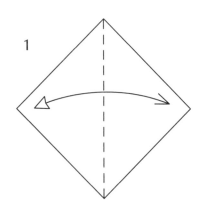

Fold and unfold.

2

Fold and unfold but
not at the corners.

3

Crease on the left.

4

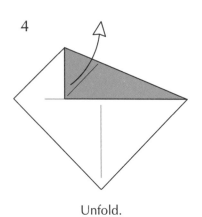

Unfold.

5

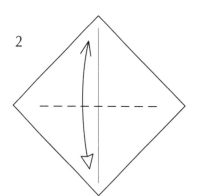

Fold and unfold
by the right.

6

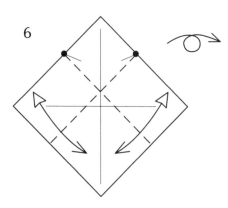

Fold and unfold.

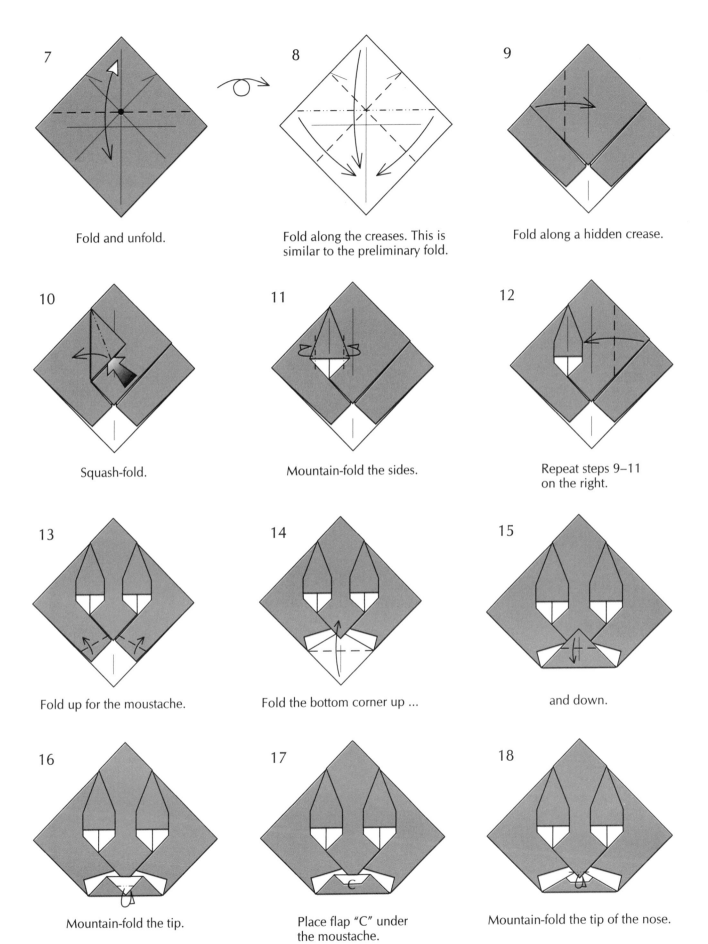

7

Fold and unfold.

8

Fold along the creases. This is similar to the preliminary fold.

9

Fold along a hidden crease.

10

Squash-fold.

11

Mountain-fold the sides.

12

Repeat steps 9–11 on the right.

13

Fold up for the moustache.

14

Fold the bottom corner up ...

15

and down.

16

Mountain-fold the tip.

17

Place flap "C" under the moustache.

18

Mountain-fold the tip of the nose.

19

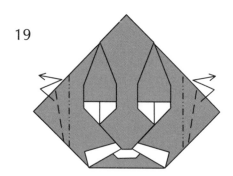

Pleat both sides to make the ears.

20

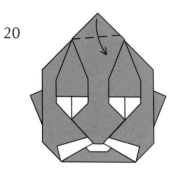

Fold down to make the hair.

21

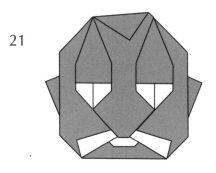

Mr. Moustache

Variation

20

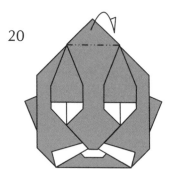

Mountain-fold the corner.

21

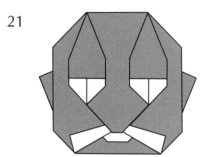

Mr. Moustache

Koi

Designed by Sipho Mabona
Switzerland

Originally diagrammed by
Sipho Mabona

This model works well by wet-folding, using paper ranging from 30 cm × 30 cm, 130 gsm to 55 cm × 55 cm, 185 gsm. Please visit Sipho Mabona's website at www.mabonaorigami.com.

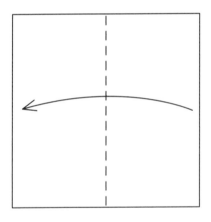

1

2

Fold and unfold.

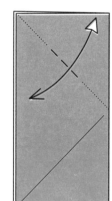

3

Fold and unfold in the center.

4

Fold and unfold on the right.

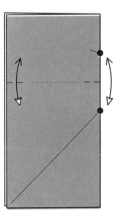

5

Fold and unfold on the left and right. The dots will meet.

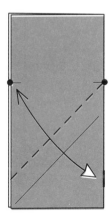

6

Fold and unfold the right edge to the dot on the left.

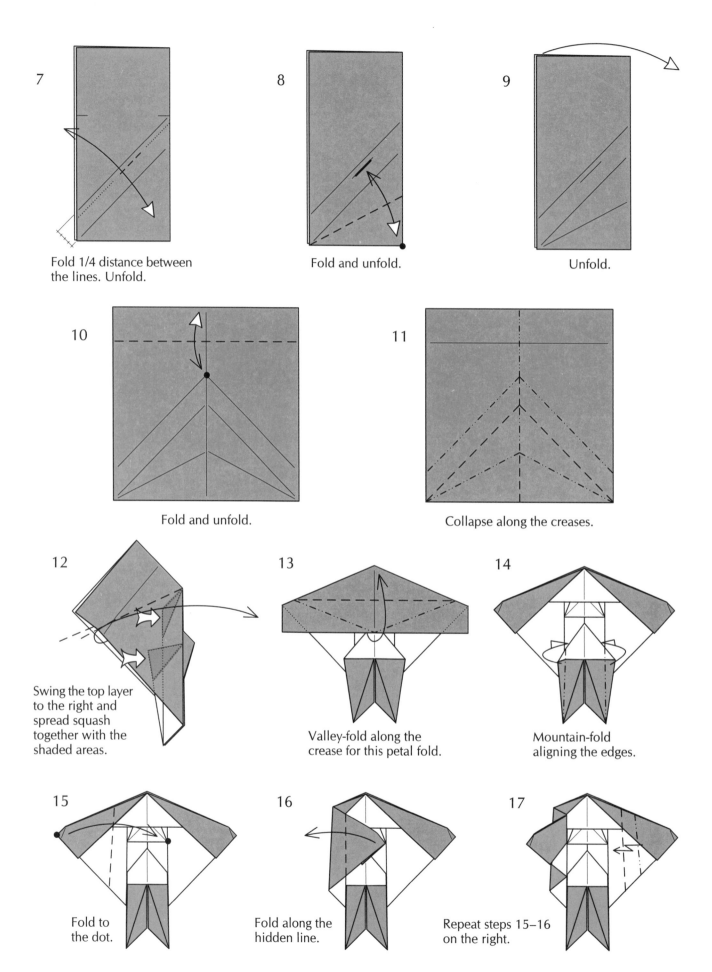

7 Fold 1/4 distance between the lines. Unfold.

8 Fold and unfold.

9 Unfold.

10 Fold and unfold.

11 Collapse along the creases.

12 Swing the top layer to the right and spread squash together with the shaded areas.

13 Valley-fold along the crease for this petal fold.

14 Mountain-fold aligning the edges.

15 Fold to the dot.

16 Fold along the hidden line.

17 Repeat steps 15–16 on the right.

18

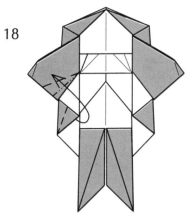

Squash-fold.

19

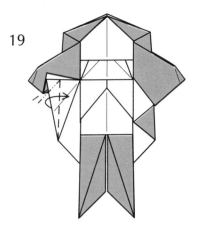

Squash-fold.

20

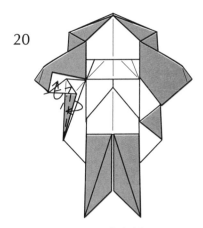

Squash-fold.

21

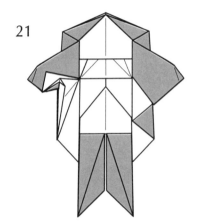

Repeat steps 18–20
on the right.

22

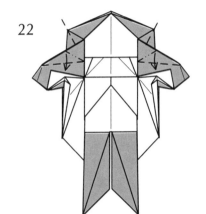

Squash folds.

23

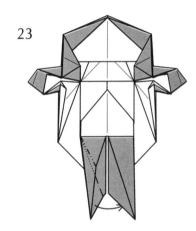

Reverse-fold so the
flap goes under the
right side.

24

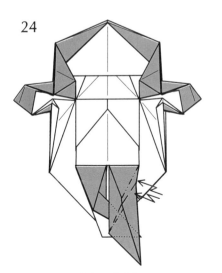

Crimp-fold.

25

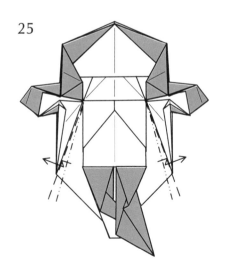

Crimp-fold. The model
will no longer lie flat.

26

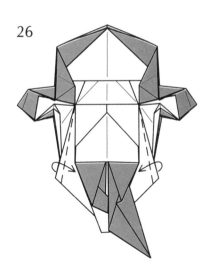

Valley-fold along the
crease made in step 25.

27

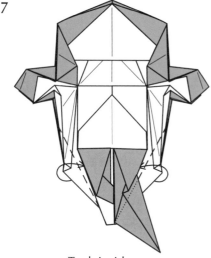

Tuck inside.

28

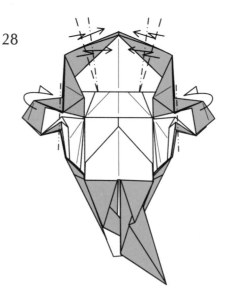

Mountain-fold the pectoral fins.
Crimp-fold the head, locking the
layers together. Steps 16–22 can
be undone for these folds.

29

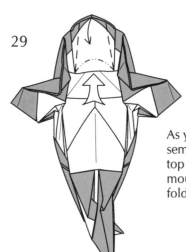

As you mountain fold the
semicircle, pull down the
top layer to open the
mouth and form valley
folds to narrow it.

30

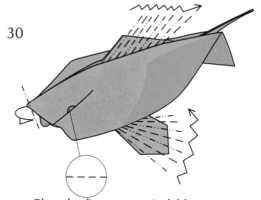

Pleat the fins, mountain-fold
the tip of the nose, and shape
the eyes and tail.

31

Koi

Elephant

Designed by Federico Scalambra
Italy

Originally diagrammed by
Federico Scalambra

I was born in 1977 in Bologna, Italy. I've been folding since I was 8 years old . I'm a member of the Centro Diffusione Origami, the Italian origami society. I love simple and funny models... like this fat elephant!

Please visit the origami group in Italy, Centro Diffusione Origami at www.origami-cdo.it/

1

Fold and unfold.

2

3

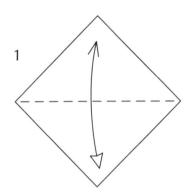

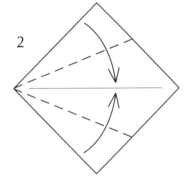

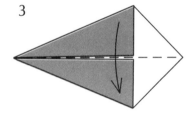

4

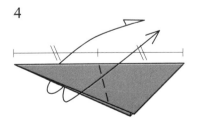

Outside-reverse-fold.

5

Outside-reverse-fold.

6

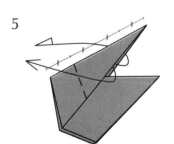

Reverse-fold the trunk. Fold and unfold on the right.

7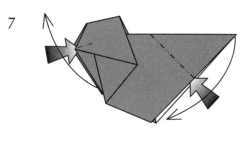

Reverse folds.

8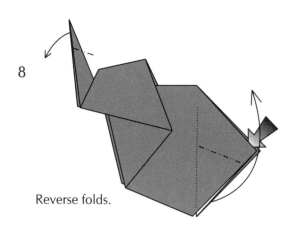

Reverse folds.

9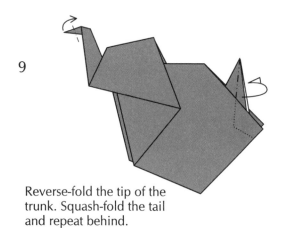

Reverse-fold the tip of the trunk. Squash-fold the tail and repeat behind.

10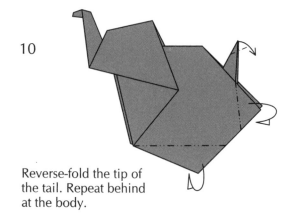

Reverse-fold the tip of the tail. Repeat behind at the body.

11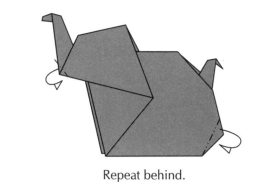

Repeat behind.

12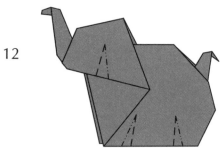

Repeat behind.

13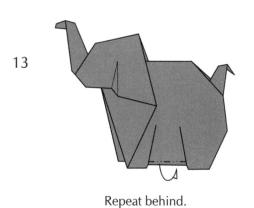

Repeat behind.

14

Elephant

Solicino

Pretty Sun

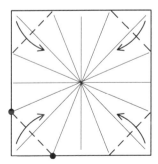

Designed by Nicoletta Maggino
Italy

Originally diagrammed by
Carlo Mugnai

Origami has always accompanied my life as a wonderful leitmotiv. Since I was a child I always folded models of other authors. One day, Pretty Sun appeared from my hands ... this increased even more my joy in making origami!

Nicoletta Maggino - Firenze - Italia
(member of CDO,
http://www.flickr.com/photos/13845707@N02/)

1
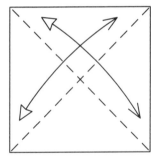

Fold and unfold.

2
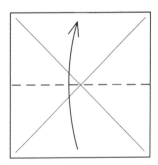

3

4
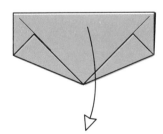

Unfold and rotate 90°.

5
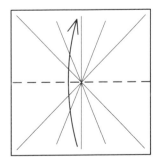

Repeat steps 2–4.

6

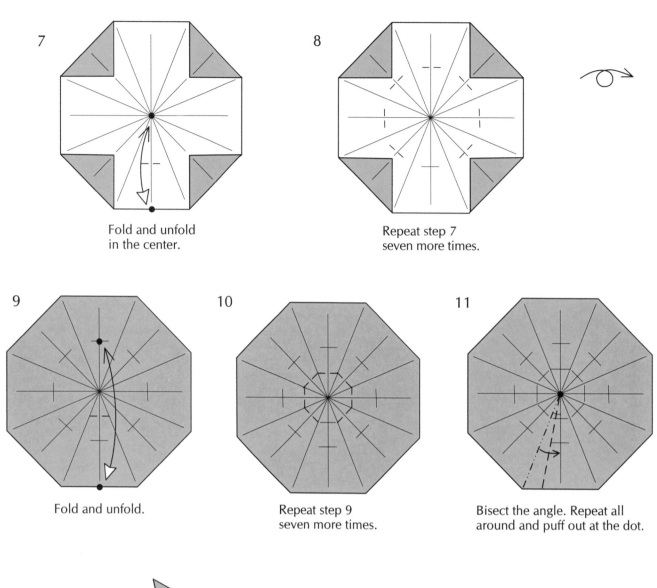

7

Fold and unfold
in the center.

8

Repeat step 7
seven more times.

9

Fold and unfold.

10

Repeat step 9
seven more times.

11

Bisect the angle. Repeat all
around and puff out at the dot.

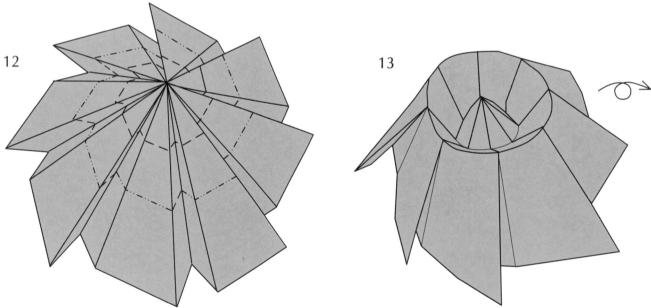

12

The model becomes 3D. Make soft, round folds, going
around concentrically, to keep the model stable.

13

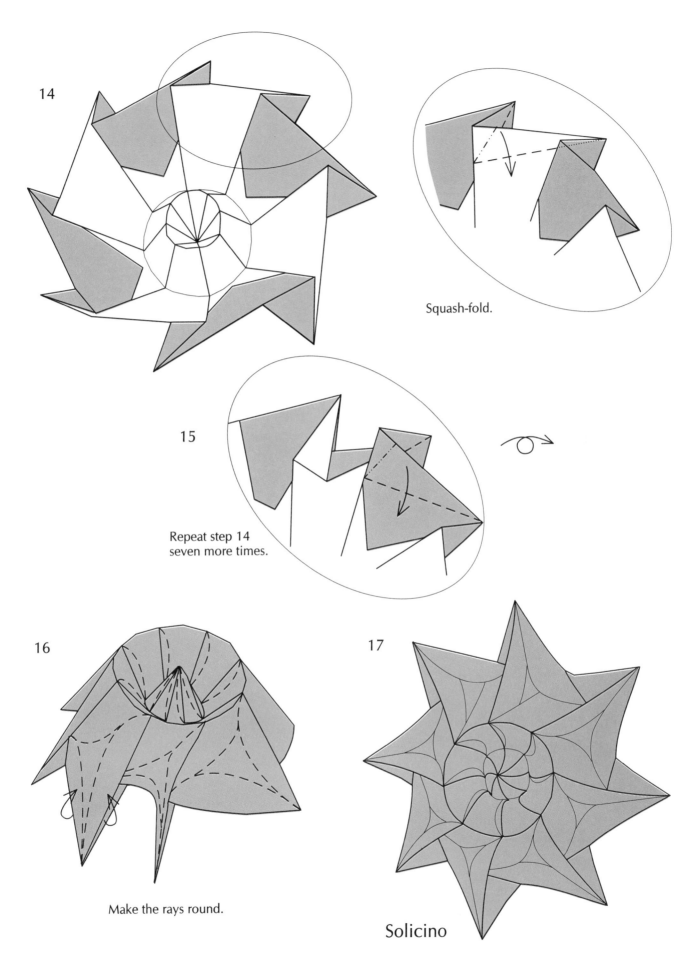

14

Squash-fold.

15

Repeat step 14
seven more times.

16

Make the rays round.

17

Solicino

Gannet

Designed by Ryan Welsh
The Netherlands

Originally diagrammed by
Ryan Welsh

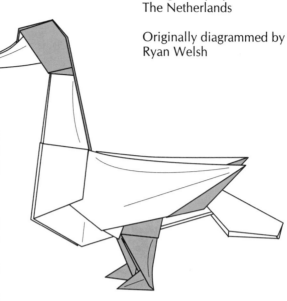

Despite being a huge fan of complex origami that requires humongous sheets of paper, over 200 steps and a tantalizing amount of patience and endurance, there is one charm that beats all others in this unique artform. Origami lets you create something stunning out of 'just' a piece of paper. I recall taking along a package of 6 inch plain kami paper and still being able to fold the universe on a train in Tuscany. In fact, I prefer designing animals that can be folded from a 6 inch sheet of plain origami paper. This gannet, that makes use of both sides of the paper, was considered lost for many years until it was rediscovered in an old box stuffed with origami doodles, when I moved to Amsterdam. It is a very distinct bird with a unique personality which it had kept after all those years in darkness. Recently, I made some minor changes in the distribution of the central layers. The bird can stand.

1

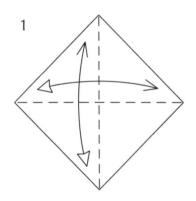

Fold and unfold.

2

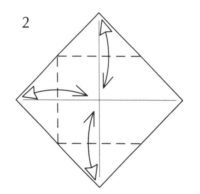

Fold and unfold.

3

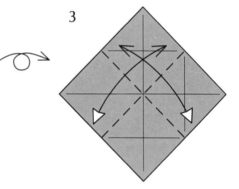

Fold and unfold.

4

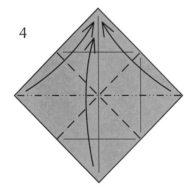

Make the Preliminary Fold.

5

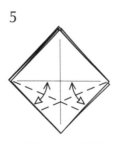

Fold and unfold.

6

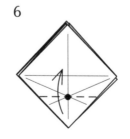

7

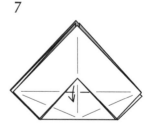

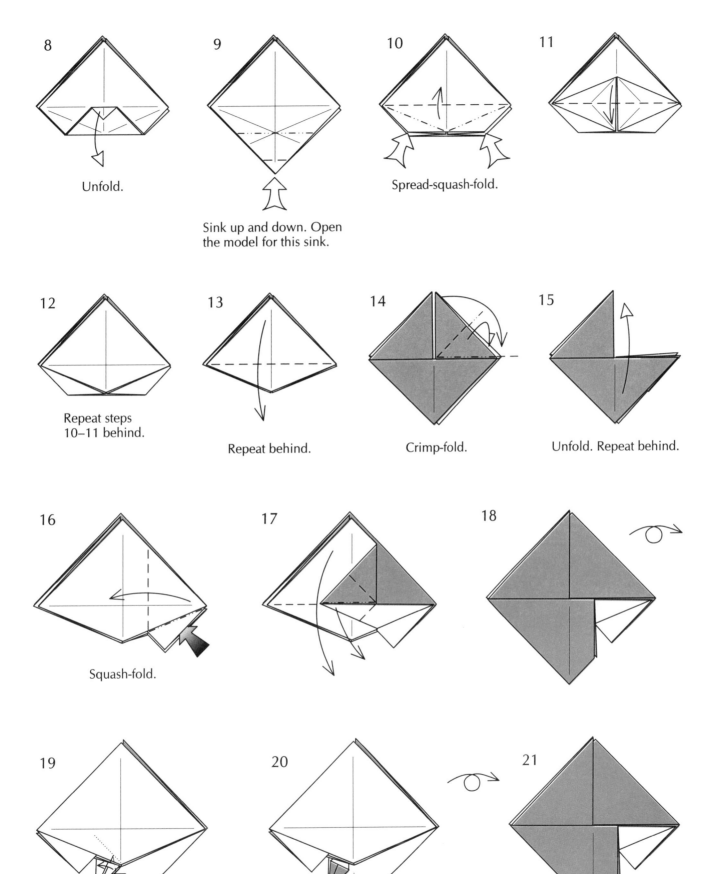

8

Unfold.

9

Sink up and down. Open
the model for this sink.

10

Spread-squash-fold.

11

12

Repeat steps
10–11 behind.

13

Repeat behind.

14

Crimp-fold.

15

Unfold. Repeat behind.

16

Squash-fold.

17

18

19

Squash-fold.

20

21

Repeat steps 16–19 behind.

Gannet 45

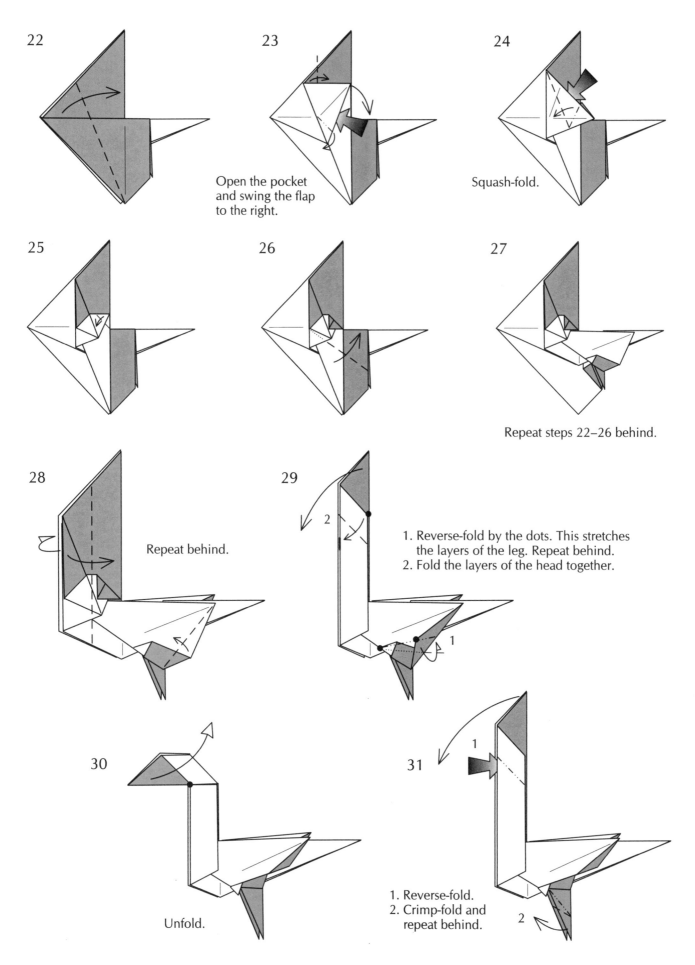

22

23

Open the pocket
and swing the flap
to the right.

24

Squash-fold.

25

26

27

Repeat steps 22–26 behind.

28

Repeat behind.

29

1. Reverse-fold by the dots. This stretches
   the layers of the leg. Repeat behind.
2. Fold the layers of the head together.

30

Unfold.

31

1. Reverse-fold.
2. Crimp-fold and
   repeat behind.

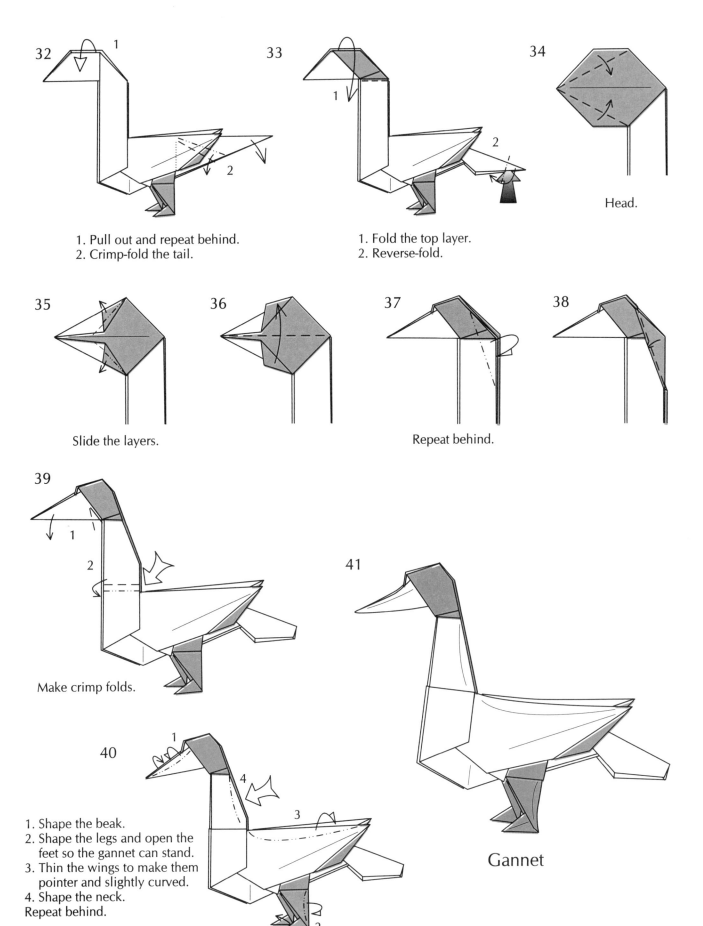

32

1. Pull out and repeat behind.
2. Crimp-fold the tail.

33

1. Fold the top layer.
2. Reverse-fold.

34

Head.

35

Slide the layers.

36

37

38

Repeat behind.

39

Make crimp folds.

40

1. Shape the beak.
2. Shape the legs and open the feet so the gannet can stand.
3. Thin the wings to make them pointer and slightly curved.
4. Shape the neck.
Repeat behind.

41

Gannet

Snail

Designed by Ryan Welsh
The Netherlands

Originally diagrammed by
Ryan Welsh

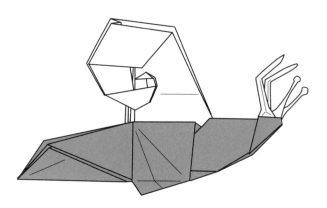

I am a huge fan of using both sides of the paper to create bicolored origami. This requires the effective use of the edges of the paper to enable the color change. This snail makes use of an off-centered Frog Base. Some of the odd looking flaps have extra paper to create the points used for the eyestalks and antennae. I am especially fond of the economical distribution of layers in the center flap and the locking mechanism of the head. Again, you should be able to fold this snail from a regular sheet of 6 inch origami paper, yet your first attempt may require a bigger sheet.

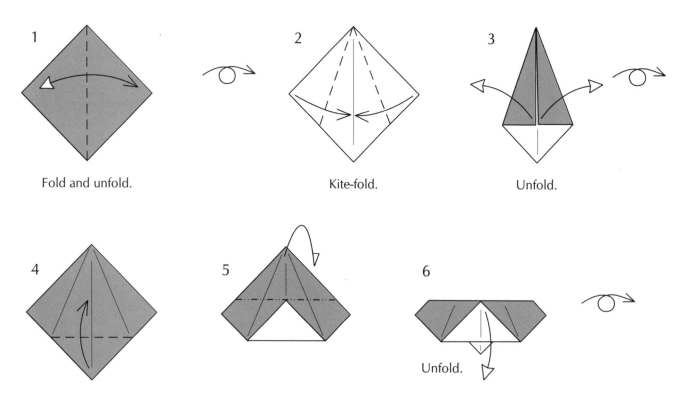

1 Fold and unfold.

2 Kite-fold.

3 Unfold.

4

5

6 Unfold.

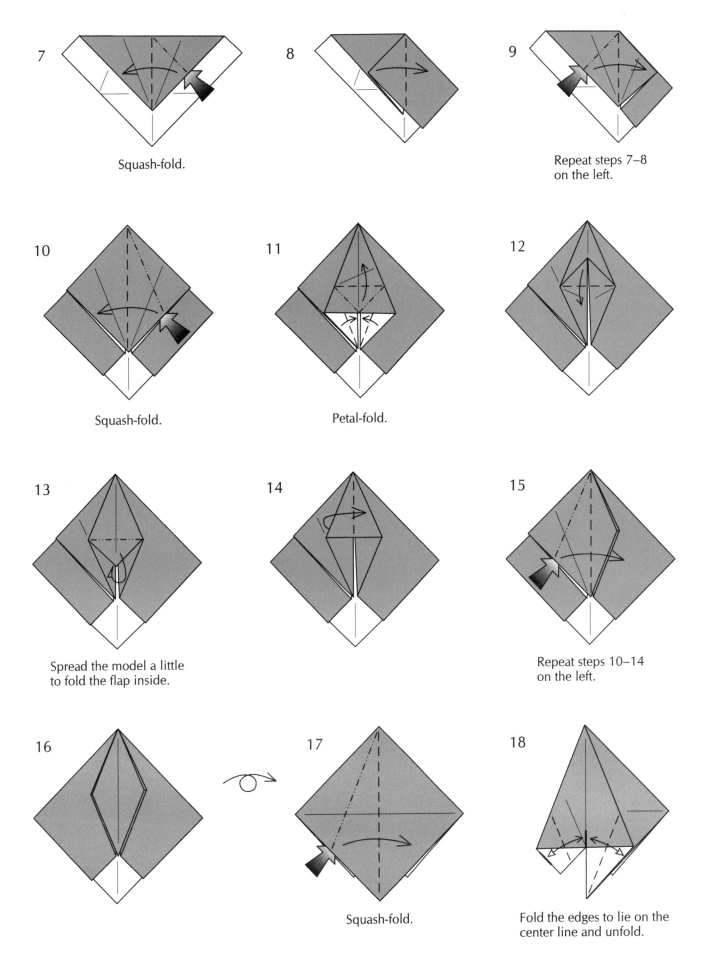

7

Squash-fold.

8

9

Repeat steps 7–8
on the left.

10

Squash-fold.

11

Petal-fold.

12

13

Spread the model a little
to fold the flap inside.

14

15

Repeat steps 10–14
on the left.

16

17

Squash-fold.

18

Fold the edges to lie on the
center line and unfold.

Snail 49

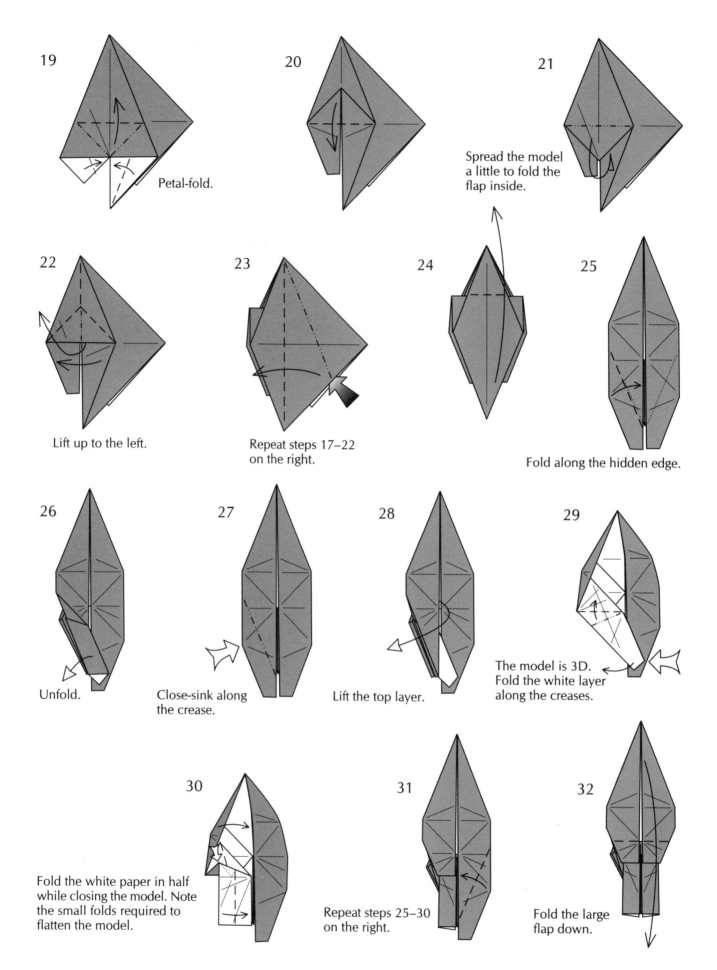

19 Petal-fold.

20

21 Spread the model a little to fold the flap inside.

22 Lift up to the left.

23 Repeat steps 17–22 on the right.

24

25 Fold along the hidden edge.

26 Unfold.

27 Close-sink along the crease.

28 Lift the top layer.

29 The model is 3D. Fold the white layer along the creases.

30 Fold the white paper in half while closing the model. Note the small folds required to flatten the model.

31 Repeat steps 25–30 on the right.

32 Fold the large flap down.

33

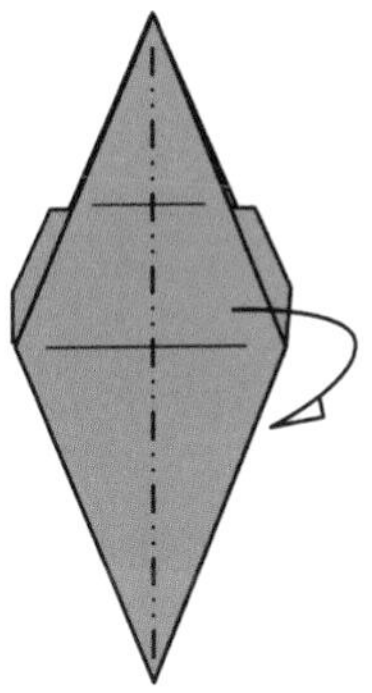

Fold in half and rotate.

34

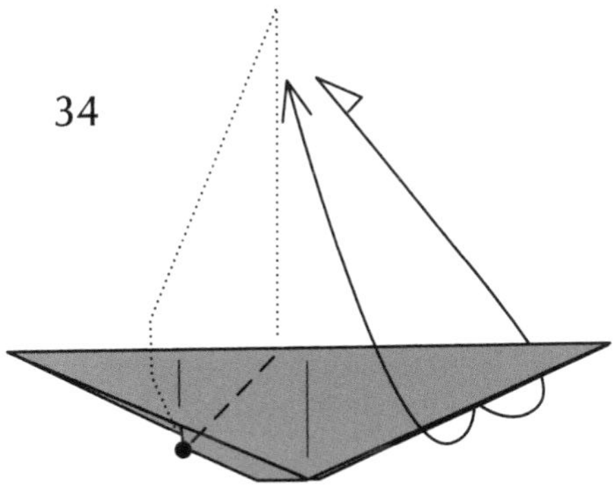

Outside-reverse-fold. Note the dotted vertical line.

35

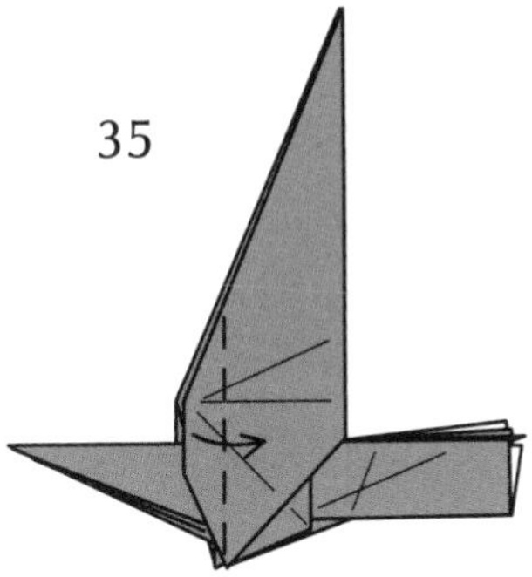

Repeat behind.

36

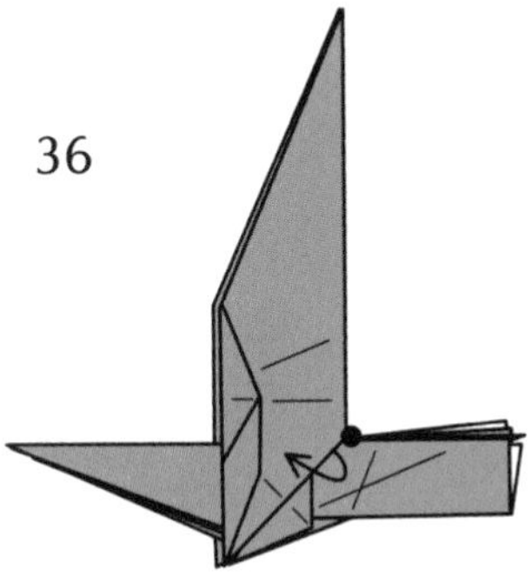

Unlock the paper at the dot. Repeat behind.

37

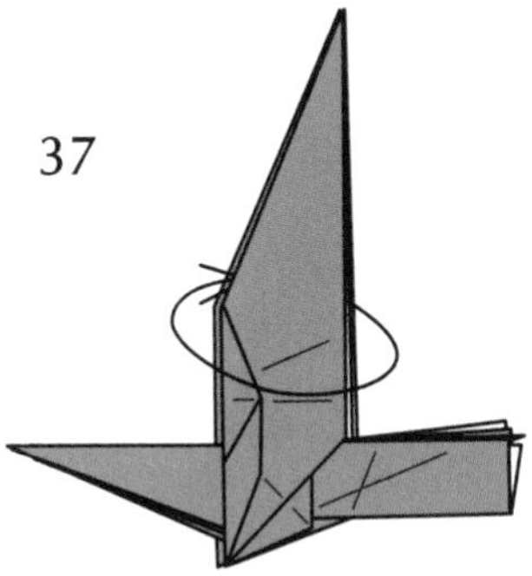

Carefully wrap one layer all around. Repeat behind.

38

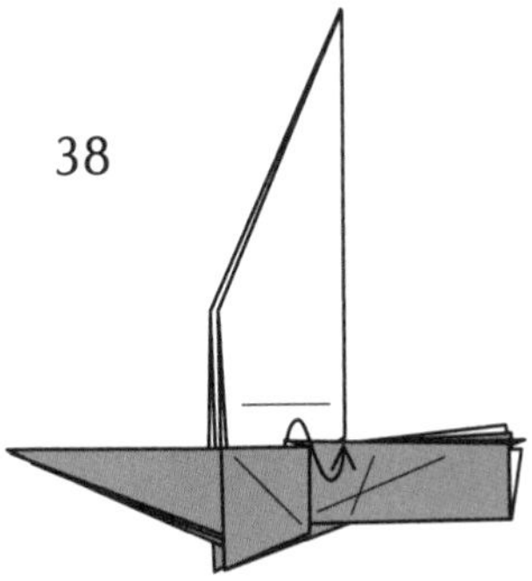

Tuck the little parallel pleat inside the pocket that lies underneath. Repeat behind.

39

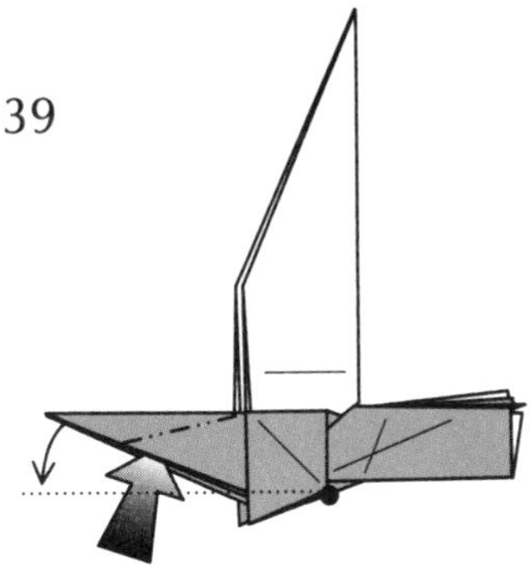

Reverse-fold so the left corner meets the dotted line.

40

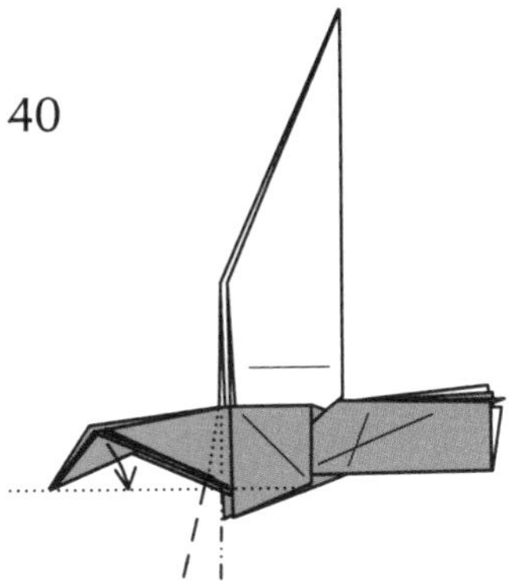

Pull out two of the four layers and pleat at the base of the point. Repeat behind.

41

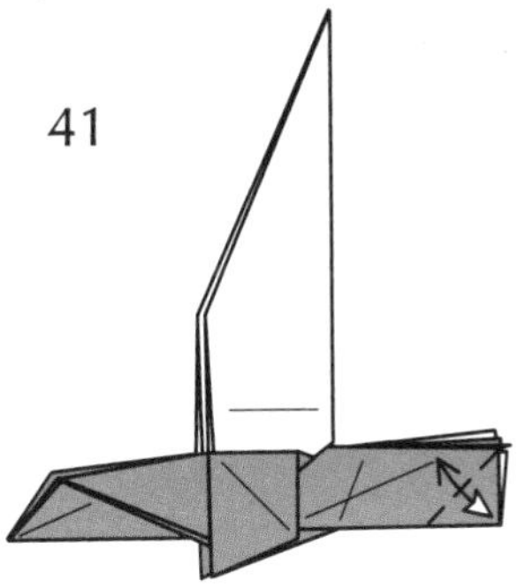

We will now work on the snail's eyestalks and antennae. Fold and unfold. Repeat behind.

42

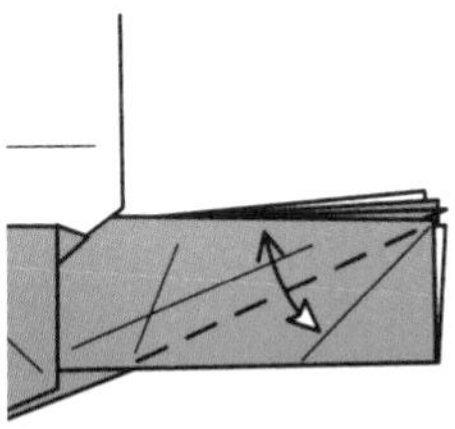

Fold and unfold.
Repeat behind.

43

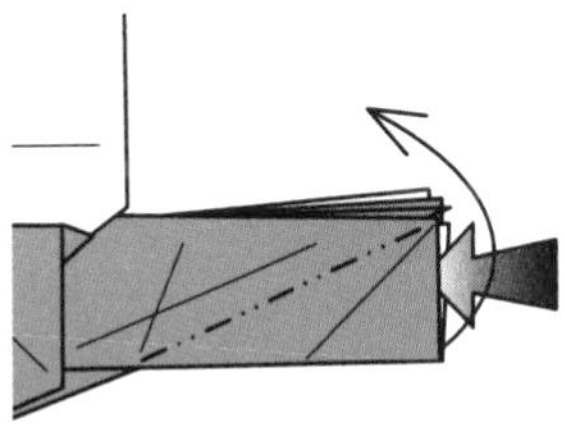

Reverse-fold.

44

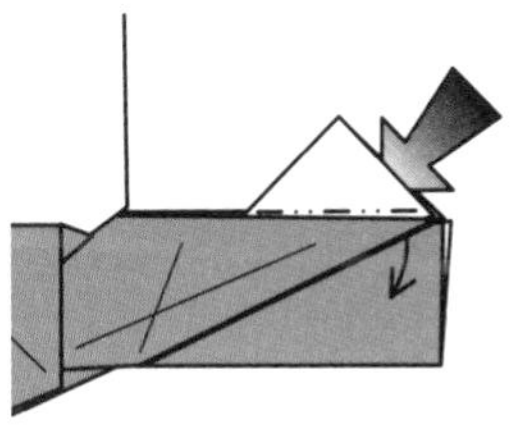

Reverse-fold.

45

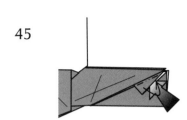

Reverse-fold.

46

Only the top part is shown in this and the next few steps. Fold the top point down perpendicular to the edge and unfold.

47

Reverse-fold.

48

Open the reverse-folded point.

49

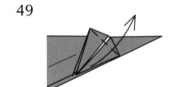

50

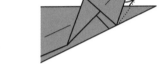

Release some trapped paper.

51

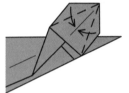

52

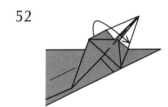

53

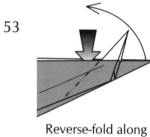

Reverse-fold along the crease.

54

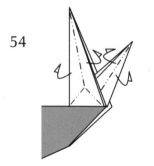

Pinch the two points.

55

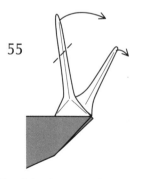

Bend the larger point to make an antennae. Open the tip of the small point to make an eyestalk.

56

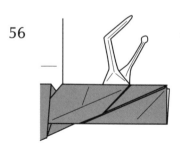

Repeat steps 43–55 behind.

57

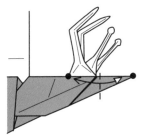

Fold and unfold.

58

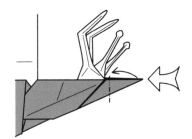

Open the paper to sink along the crease.

59

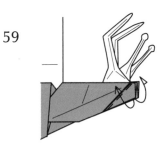

Note the edges on the right form a "W". Outside-reverse-fold around the layers of the antennae and eyestalks to keep them in place.

60

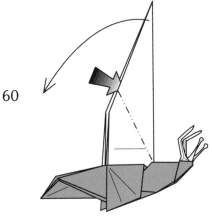

Reverse-fold.

61

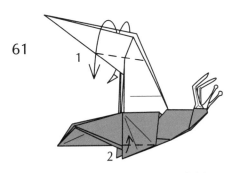

1. Outside-reverse-fold.
2. Repeat behind.

62

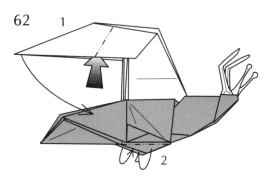

1. Reverse-fold/close-sink.
2. Fold the inner layers.

63

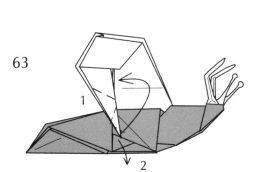

1. Continue reverse folding the shell.
2. Fold the corner out and repeat behind.

64

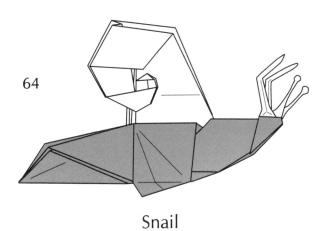

Snail

Heart in Heart

Designed by Helen Lee
Canada

Please visit tsunori.net.

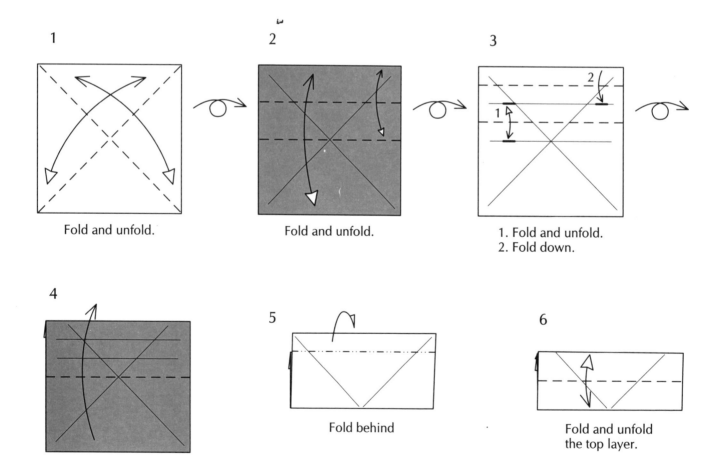

1

Fold and unfold.

2

Fold and unfold.

3

1. Fold and unfold.
2. Fold down.

4

5

Fold behind

6

Fold and unfold
the top layer.

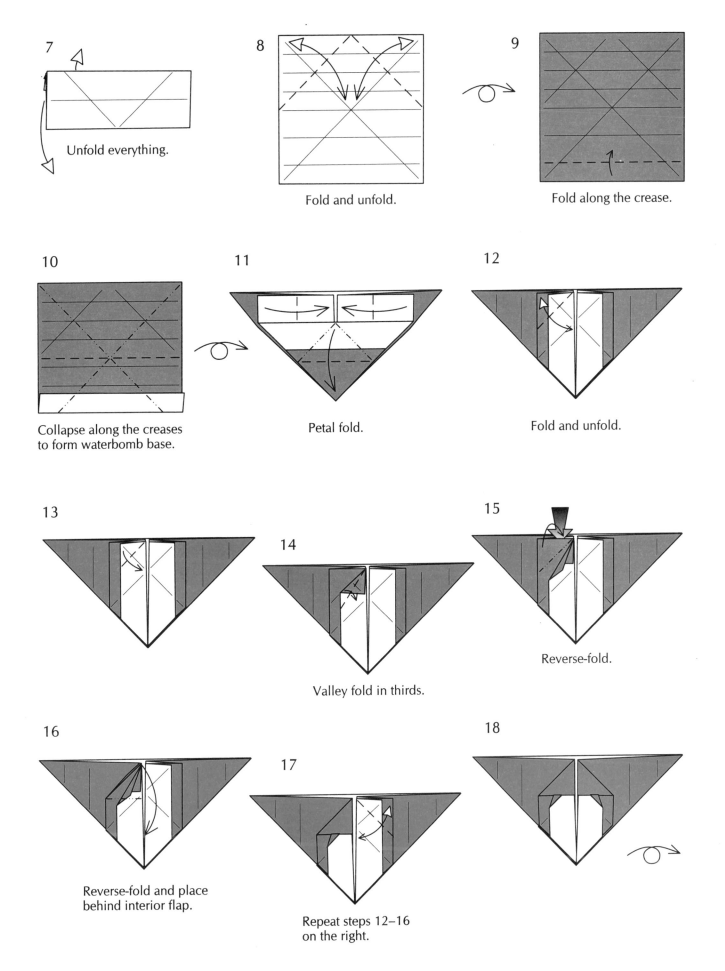

7

Unfold everything.

8

Fold and unfold.

9

Fold along the crease.

10

Collapse along the creases
to form waterbomb base.

11

Petal fold.

12

Fold and unfold.

13

14

Valley fold in thirds.

15

Reverse-fold.

16

Reverse-fold and place
behind interior flap.

17

Repeat steps 12–16
on the right.

18

Heart in Heart 55

19

Petal-fold.

20

Squash-fold.
Repeat on right.

21

22

Reverse-fold. Repeat on
right. Fold bottom up.

23

Fold to center.

24

Reverse-fold.
Repeat on right.

25

26

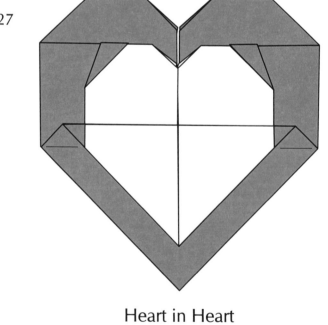

27

Heart in Heart

Diver Down Flag

Designed by Brian K. Webb
United States of America

Please visit Brian K. Webb's origami publishing
website at www.eorigamipublishing.com

1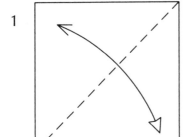

Fold and unfold.

2

Fold and unfold
on the edges.

3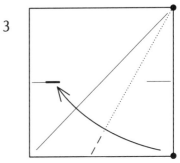

Bring the corner to the
crease. Fold on the bottom.

4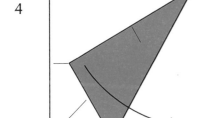

Unfold.

5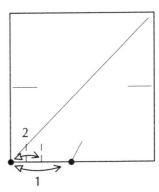

Fold and unfold in half twice,
creasing on the bottom.

6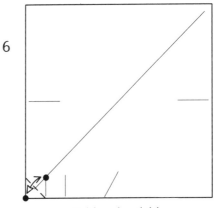

Fold and unfold.
Rotate 180°.

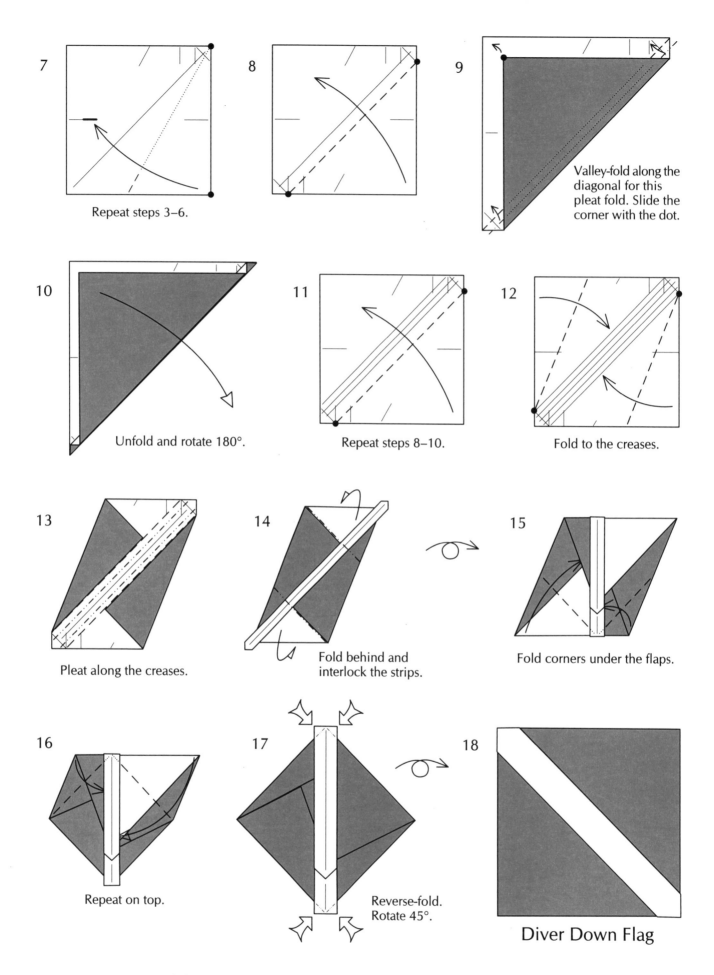

7 Repeat steps 3–6.

8

9 Valley-fold along the diagonal for this pleat fold. Slide the corner with the dot.

10 Unfold and rotate 180°.

11 Repeat steps 8–10.

12 Fold to the creases.

13 Pleat along the creases.

14 Fold behind and interlock the strips.

15 Fold corners under the flaps.

16 Repeat on top.

17 Reverse-fold. Rotate 45°.

18 Diver Down Flag

Santa

Designed by Brian K. Webb
United States of America

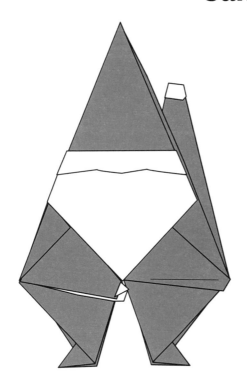

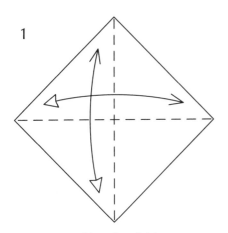

1

Fold and unfold.

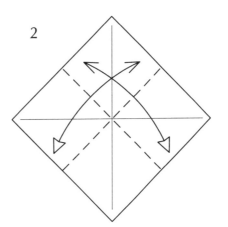

2

Fold and unfold.

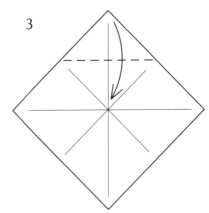

3

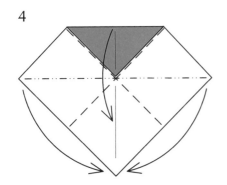

4

Collapse along
existing creases.

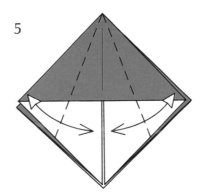

5

Fold and unfold.

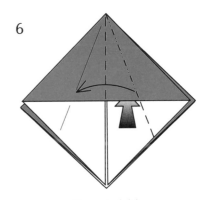

6

Squash-fold.

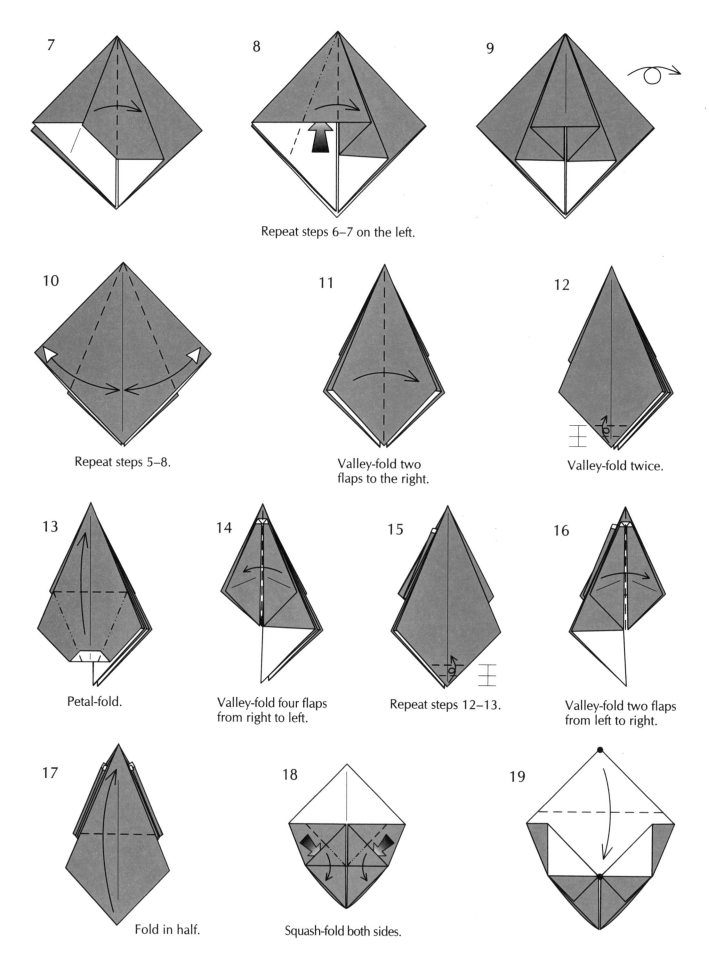

7

8

Repeat steps 6–7 on the left.

9

10

Repeat steps 5–8.

11

Valley-fold two
flaps to the right.

12

Valley-fold twice.

13

Petal-fold.

14

Valley-fold four flaps
from right to left.

15

Repeat steps 12–13.

16

Valley-fold two flaps
from left to right.

17

Fold in half.

18

Squash-fold both sides.

19

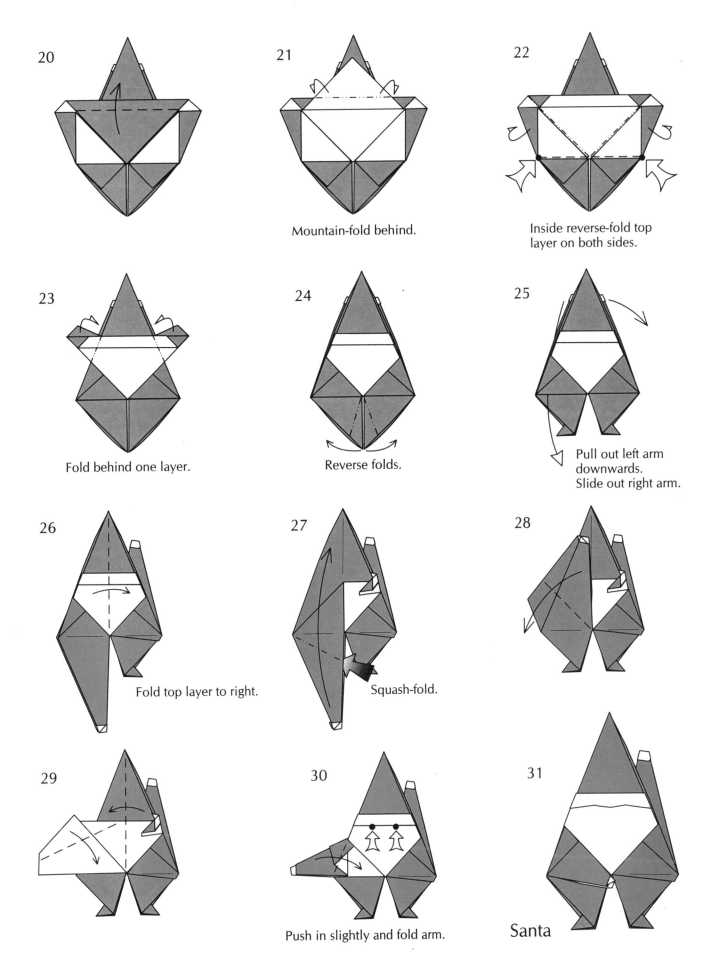

20

21
Mountain-fold behind.

22
Inside reverse-fold top
layer on both sides.

23
Fold behind one layer.

24
Reverse folds.

25
Pull out left arm
downwards.
Slide out right arm.

26
Fold top layer to right.

27
Squash-fold.

28

29

30
Push in slightly and fold arm.

31
Santa

Rhinoceros

Designed by John Montroll
United States of America

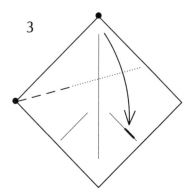

One summer, I would visit a neighbor quite often because she delighted in teaching me origami. I was four, and have no memory of that. I do recall collecting origami books when I was six. During the years, I was interested in designing models where each was folded from one uncut square, with a certain amount of detail. This was against the norm of that generation. I now have created a large collection of origami birds, animals, dinosaurs, along with polyhedra and other geometrics. I have also witnessed an impressive developement throughout the entire origami world.

Please visit www.johnmontroll.com.

1

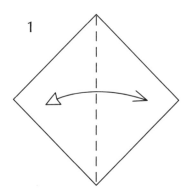

Fold and unfold.

2

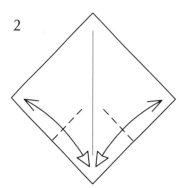

Fold and unfold.

3

Bring the top corner to the line and crease on the left.

4

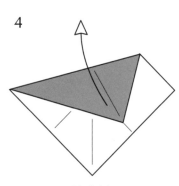

Unfold.

5

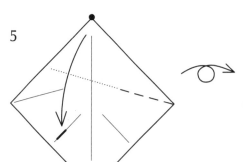

Repeat steps 3–4 on the right.

6

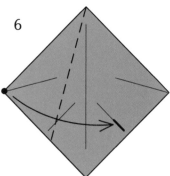

Bring the corner to the line.

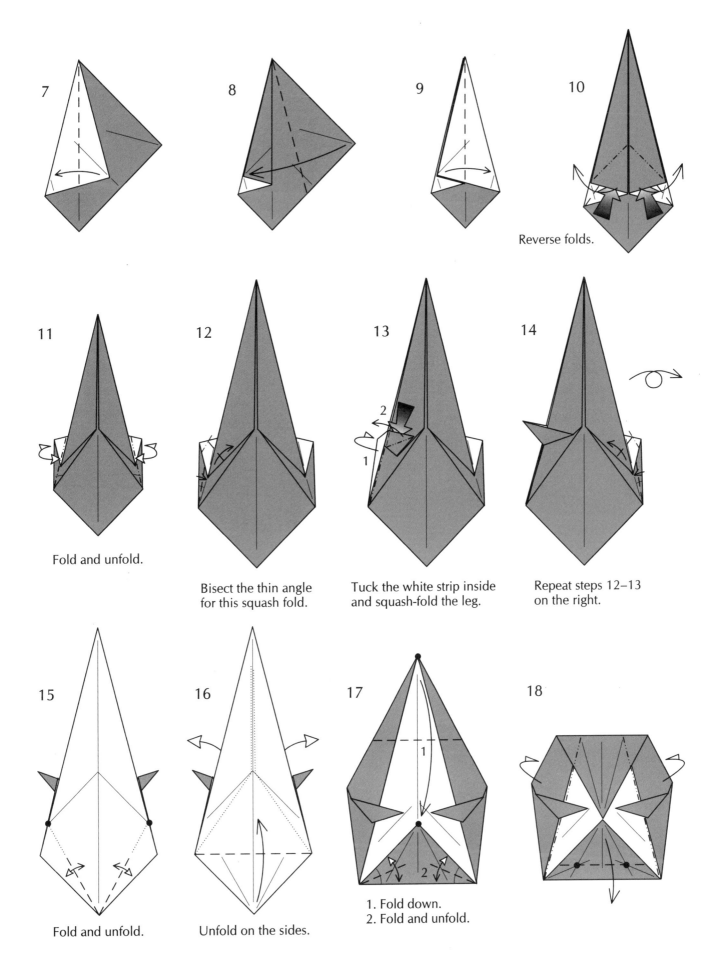

7

8

9

10

Reverse folds.

11

Fold and unfold.

12

Bisect the thin angle
for this squash fold.

13

Tuck the white strip inside
and squash-fold the leg.

14

Repeat steps 12–13
on the right.

15

Fold and unfold.

16

Unfold on the sides.

17

1. Fold down.
2. Fold and unfold.

18

19

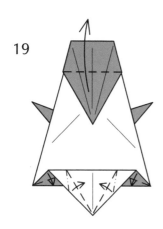

Make squash folds at the tail.

20

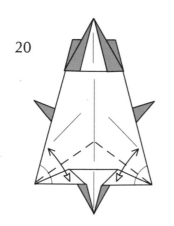

Fold and unfold to bisect the angle.

21

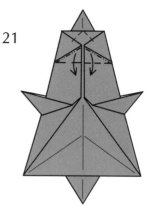

Squash folds.

22

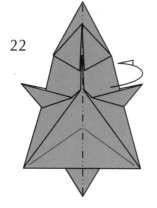

Fold in half and rotate.

23

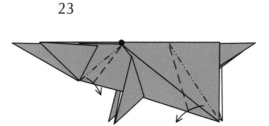

Crimp-fold at the neck and hind legs.

24

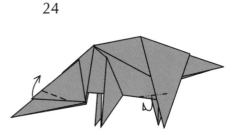

1. Outside-reverse-fold.
2. Squash-fold. Repeat behind.

25

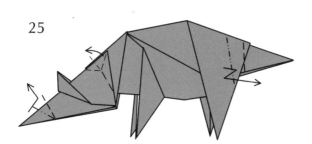

Crimp-fold the horn and tail. Rabbit-ear the ear and repeat behind.

26

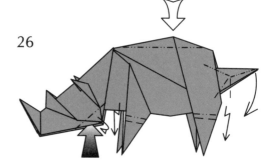

Double-rabbit-ear the tail. Crimp-fold the legs. Reverse-fold the head. Sink the back. Repeat behind.

27

Crimp-fold the horn, outside-reverse-fold the tail, reverse and crimp-fold the feet, fold behind at the neck, open the ears, and shape the back. Repeat behind.

28

Rhinoceros

Hot Air Balloon

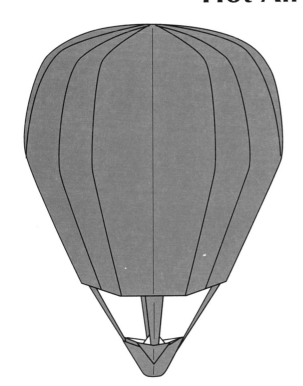

Designed by John Szinger
United States of America

Originally diagrammed by
John Szinger

John Szinger is an American origami artist living in New York. His approach synthesizes a range of techniques to achieve a dimensional, stylized realism that evokes a classic, essential simplicity. His inspiration comes from a variety of sources. Favorite subjects include animals, vehicles, polyhedra, and abstract geometric patterns. The Hot Air Balloon shows his fascination with curved, voluminous forms. John is also an accomplished musician.

You can see more of John's work at http://zingorigami.com

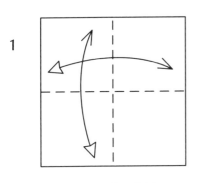

1

Fold and unfold.

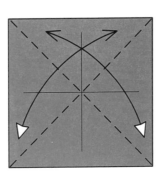

2

Fold and unfold.

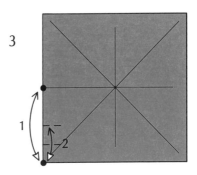

3

Fold and unfold to find the 1/8 mark.

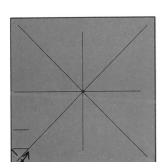

4

Fold to the crease. Rotate 90°.

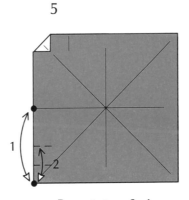

5

Repeat steps 3–4 three more times.

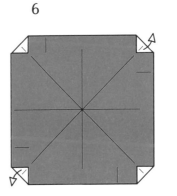

6

Unfold two opposite corners.

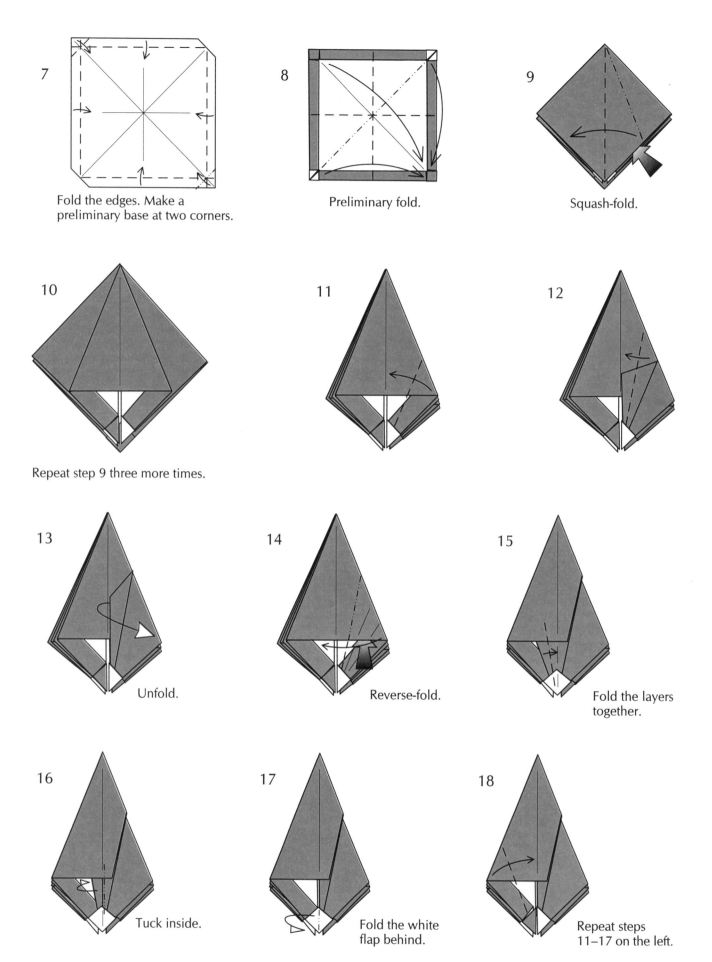

7 Fold the edges. Make a preliminary base at two corners.

8 Preliminary fold.

9 Squash-fold.

10 Repeat step 9 three more times.

11

12

13 Unfold.

14 Reverse-fold.

15 Fold the layers together.

16 Tuck inside.

17 Fold the white flap behind.

18 Repeat steps 11–17 on the left.

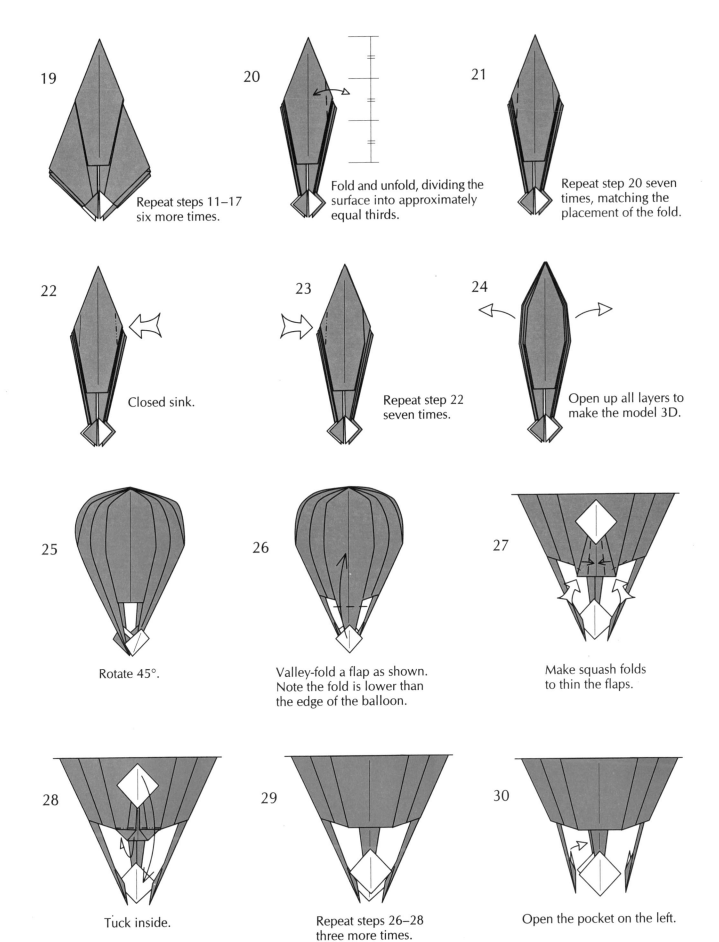

19

Repeat steps 11–17 six more times.

20

Fold and unfold, dividing the surface into approximately equal thirds.

21

Repeat step 20 seven times, matching the placement of the fold.

22

Closed sink.

23

Repeat step 22 seven times.

24

Open up all layers to make the model 3D.

25

Rotate 45°.

26

Valley-fold a flap as shown. Note the fold is lower than the edge of the balloon.

27

Make squash folds to thin the flaps.

28

Tuck inside.

29

Repeat steps 26–28 three more times.

30

Open the pocket on the left.

Hot Air Balloon 67

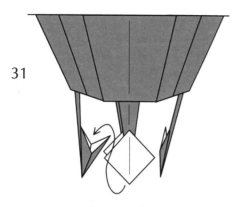

31

Put the two white flaps
together and fit them
into the left flap.

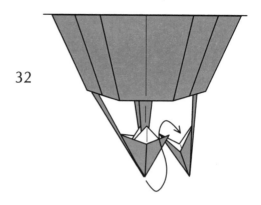

32

Slide the three flaps
together into the right
flap to form the basket.

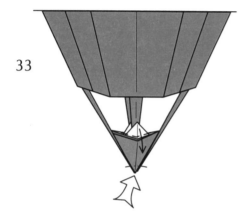

33

Valley-fold the corner to lock
the flaps together. Repeat
behind. Push in at the bottom.

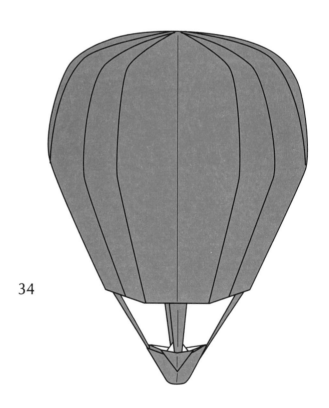

34

Hot Air Balloon

Tropical Morpho Butterfly

Designed by Robert J. Lang
United States of America

Originally diagrammed by
Robert J. Lang

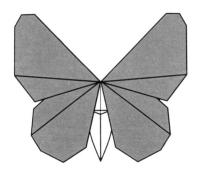

Please visit Robert Lang's website at
www.langorigami.com

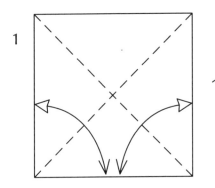

1

Fold and unfold along both diagonals.

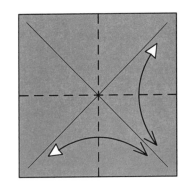

2

Fold and unfold.

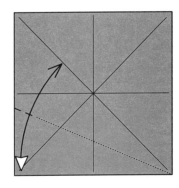

3

Fold the bottom edge up to lie along
the diagonal; make a pinch along
the left edge and unfold.

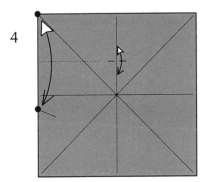

4

Fold the top left corner down to the
mark; make a pinch in the center of
the folded edge and unfold.

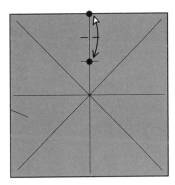

5

Fold the top edge down to the mark;
make another pinch in the center of
the folded edge and unfold.

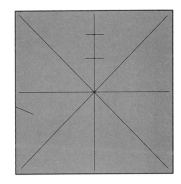

6

Rotate 180°.

7

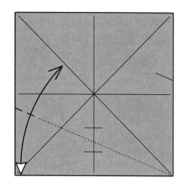

Repeat steps 3–5. Then
rotate the paper 1/8 turn.

8

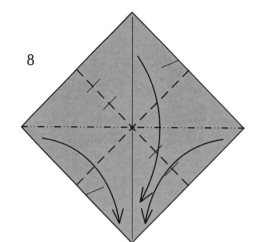

Fold a Preliminary Fold
from the existing creases.

9

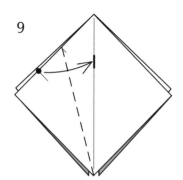

Fold one flap over so that the
indicated mark lands on the
center line of the model.

10

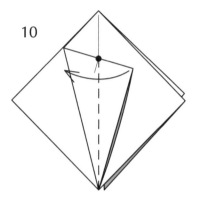

Fold the flap back to the
left along the center line.

11

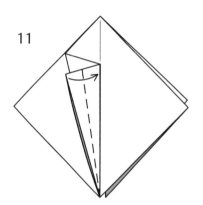

Fold the flap back in
to the center line.

12

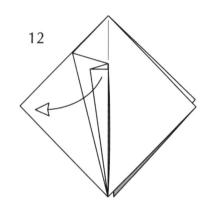

Unfold to step 9.

13

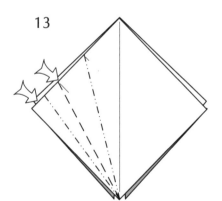

Reverse-fold in and out
on the existing creases.

14

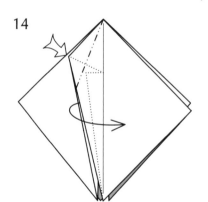

Spread-sink the corner
symmetrically.

15

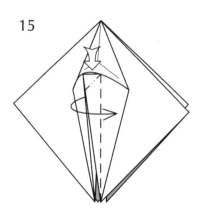

In progress. Spread-sink the
corner inside symmetrically
as well.

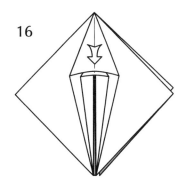

16

Flatten completely.

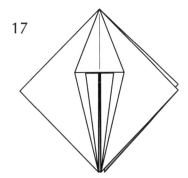

17

In a stroke of incredible karmic confluence, the two horizontal edges line up perfectly. Repeat steps 9–16 behind.

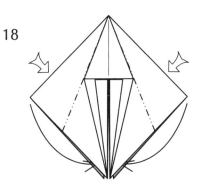

18

Reverse-fold the side edges in to the center line.

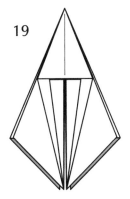

19

Rotate 180°.

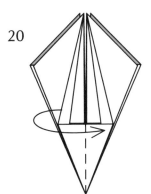

20

Fold one layer to the right.

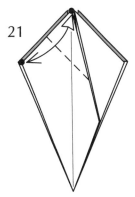

21

Fold the top corner down to the side corner and unfold.

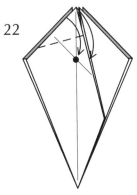

22

Fold the top corner down so that the raw edge hits the dot and the right edges of the flap are aligned.

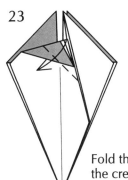

23

Fold the corner down along the crease you made in step 20, folding through all layers.

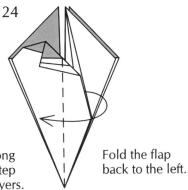

24

Fold the flap back to the left.

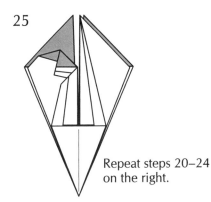

25

Repeat steps 20–24 on the right.

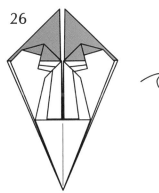

26

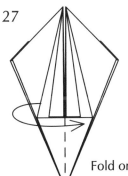

27

Fold one layer to the right.

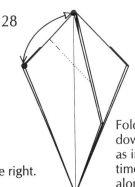

28

Fold the top corner down to the side corner as in step 21, but this time only make a pinch along the edge.

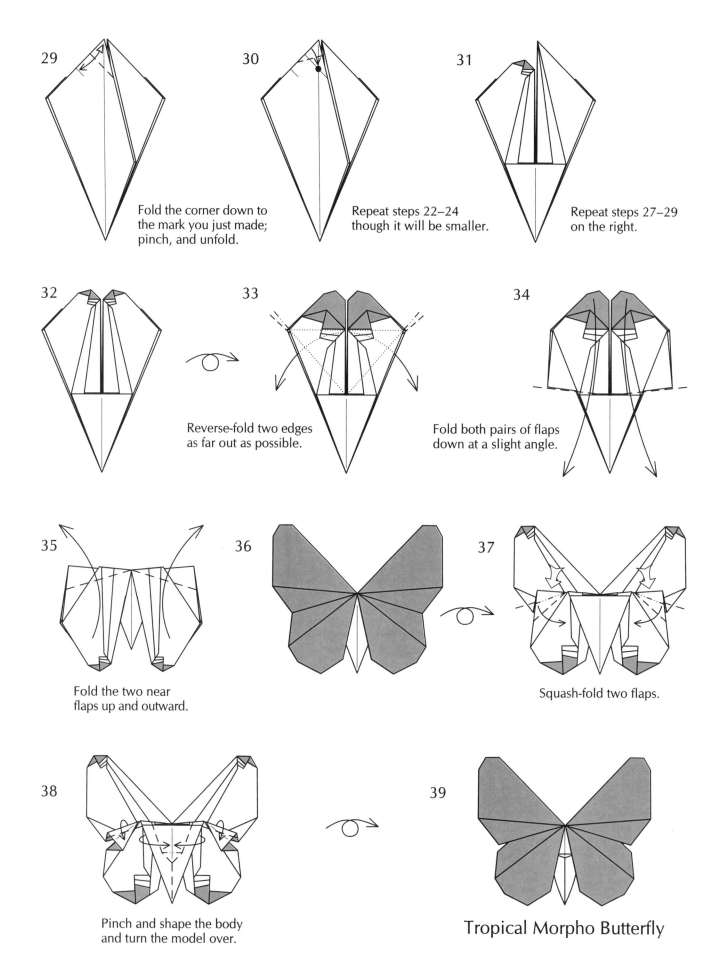

29 Fold the corner down to the mark you just made; pinch, and unfold.

30 Repeat steps 22–24 though it will be smaller.

31 Repeat steps 27–29 on the right.

32

33 Reverse-fold two edges as far out as possible.

34 Fold both pairs of flaps down at a slight angle.

35 Fold the two near flaps up and outward.

36

37 Squash-fold two flaps.

38 Pinch and shape the body and turn the model over.

39 Tropical Morpho Butterfly

Toucan

Designed by Miguel A. Callisaya
Bolivia

Originally diagrammed by
Miguel A. Callisaya

Please visit http://origamibolivia.blogspot.com/

1

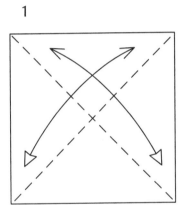

Fold and unfold.

2

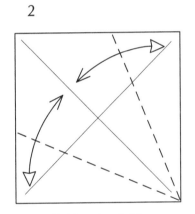

Fold and unfold.

3

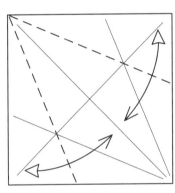

Fold and unfold.

4

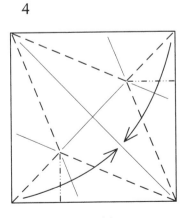

Make two rabbit ears.

5

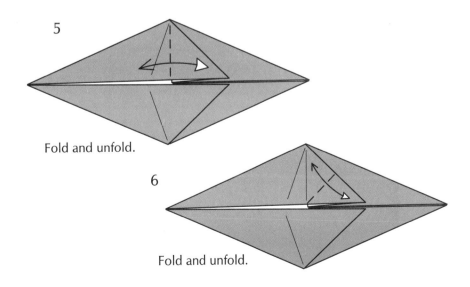

Fold and unfold.

6

Fold and unfold.

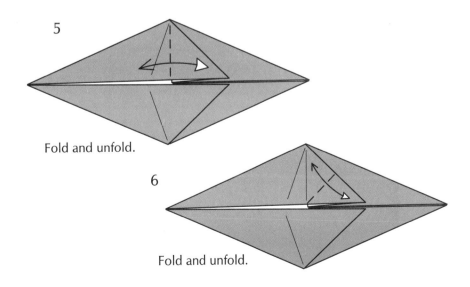

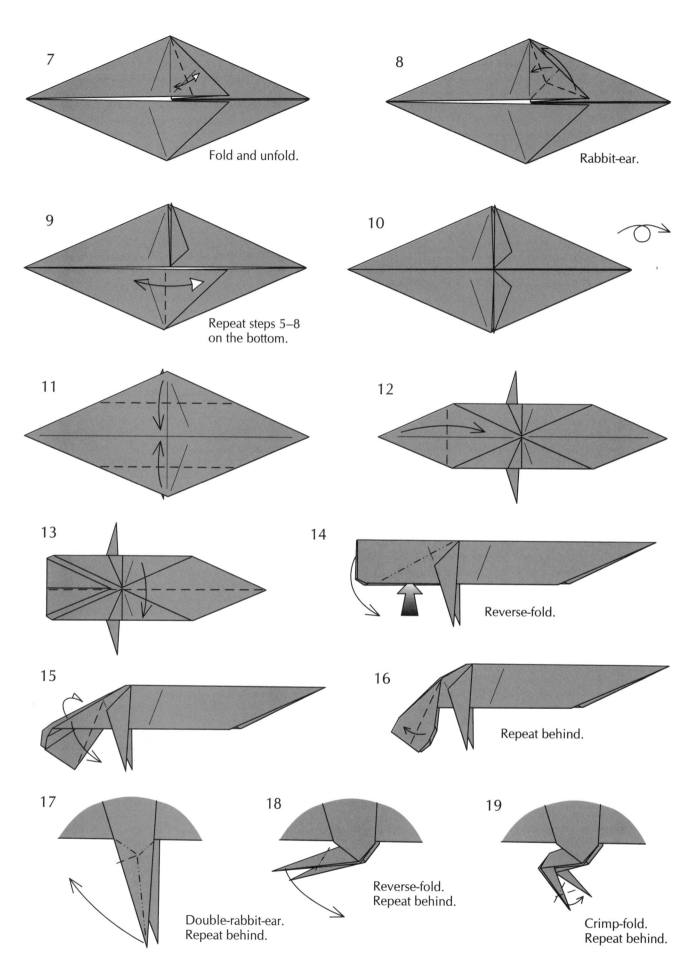

7 Fold and unfold.

8 Rabbit-ear.

9 Repeat steps 5–8 on the bottom.

10

11

12

13

14 Reverse-fold.

15

16 Repeat behind.

17 Double-rabbit-ear. Repeat behind.

18 Reverse-fold. Repeat behind.

19 Crimp-fold. Repeat behind.

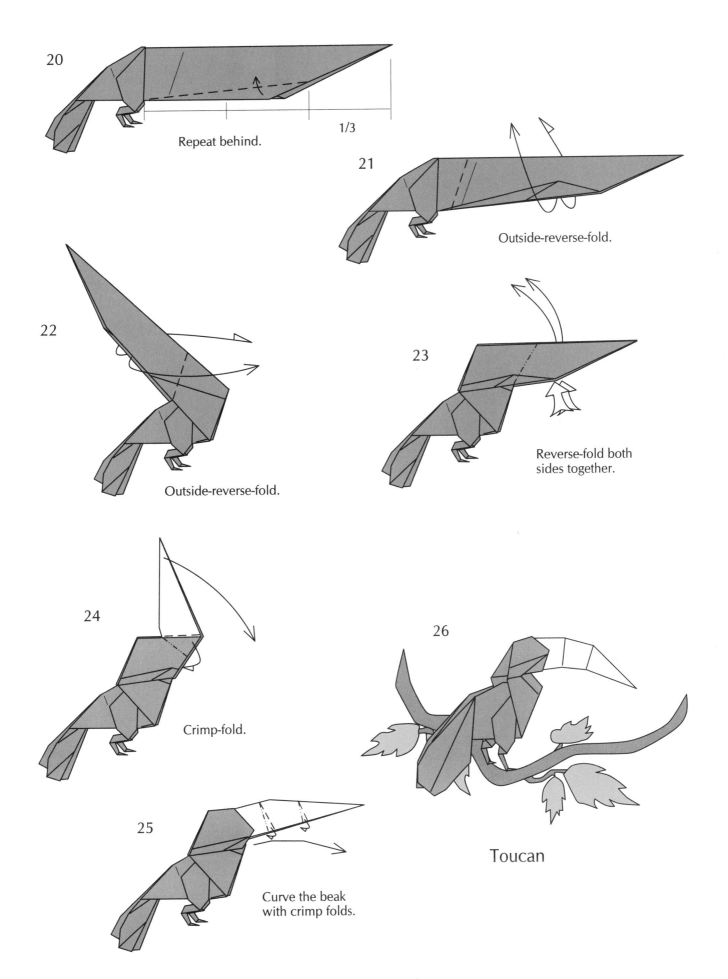

20

Repeat behind.

1/3

21

Outside-reverse-fold.

22

Outside-reverse-fold.

23

Reverse-fold both
sides together.

24

Crimp-fold.

25

Curve the beak
with crimp folds.

26

Toucan

Crocodile

Designed by Patricio Kunz Tomic
Chile

Originally diagrammed by Patricio
Kunz Tomic

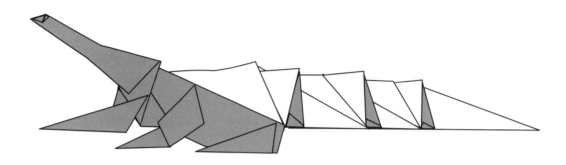

Please visit www.origamichile.cl.

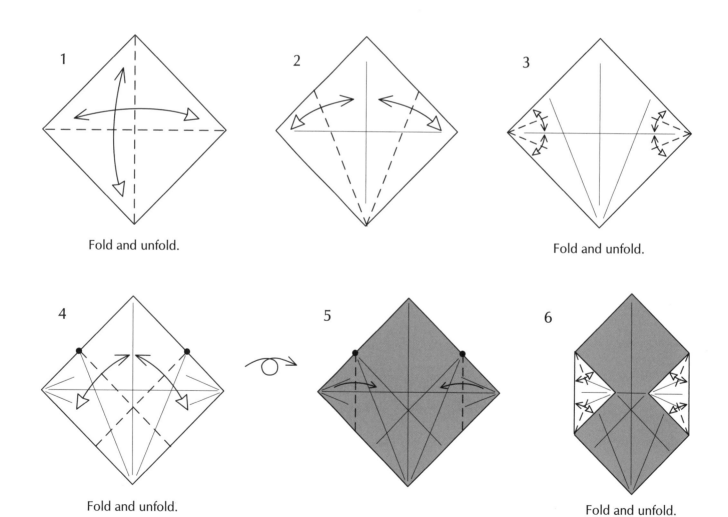

1

Fold and unfold.

2

3

Fold and unfold.

4

Fold and unfold.

5

6

Fold and unfold.

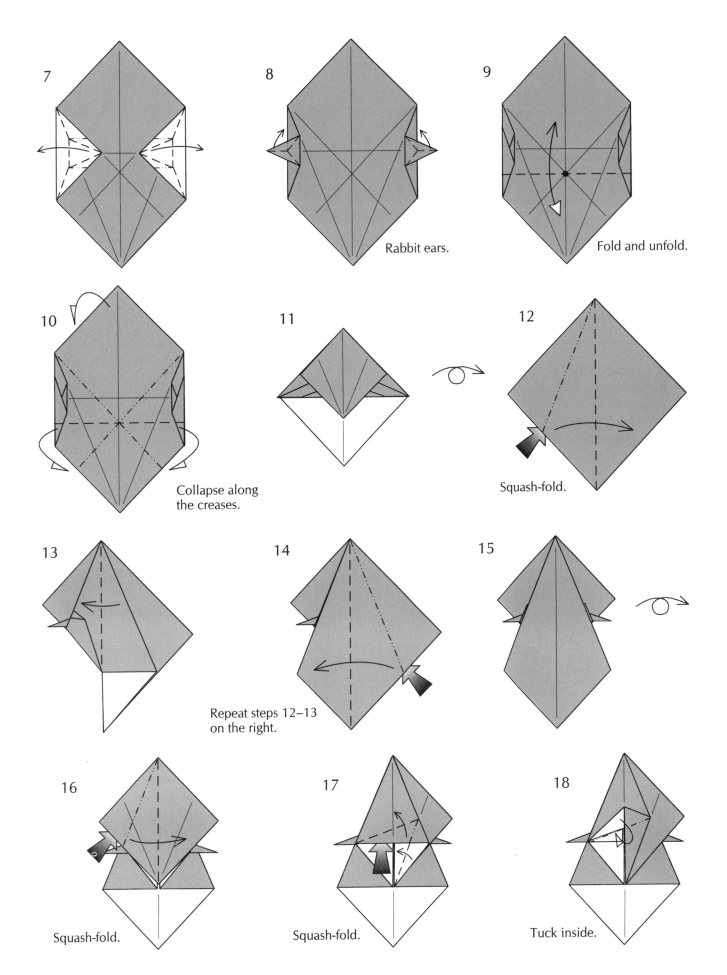

7

8

Rabbit ears.

9

Fold and unfold.

10

Collapse along the creases.

11

12

Squash-fold.

13

14

Repeat steps 12–13 on the right.

15

16

Squash-fold.

17

Squash-fold.

18

Tuck inside.

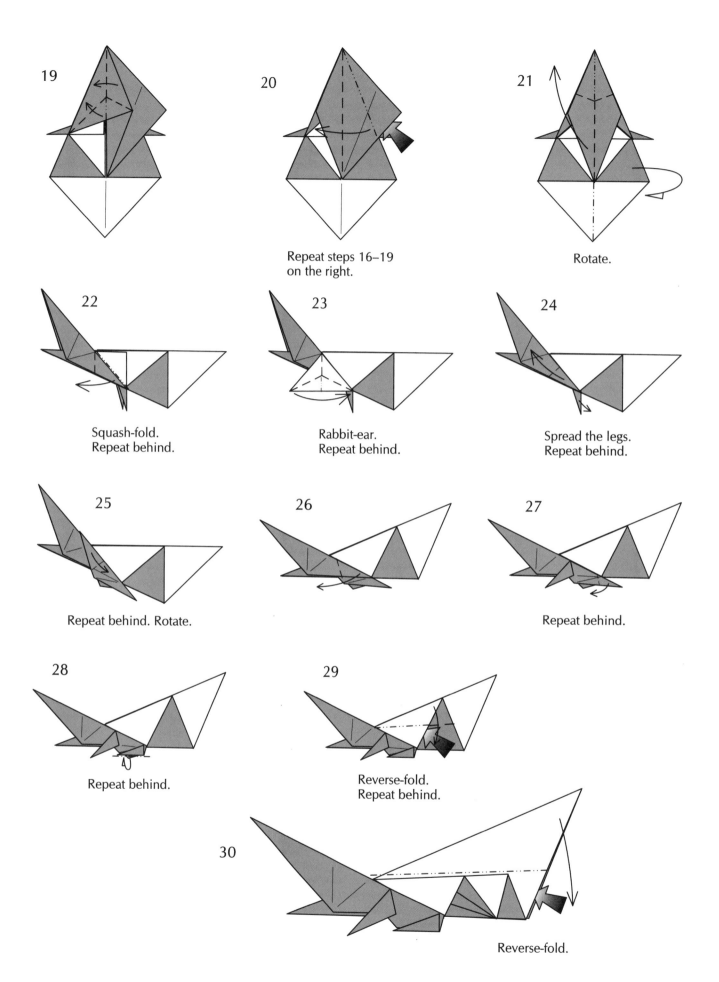

19

20

Repeat steps 16–19
on the right.

21

Rotate.

22

Squash-fold.
Repeat behind.

23

Rabbit-ear.
Repeat behind.

24

Spread the legs.
Repeat behind.

25

Repeat behind. Rotate.

26

27

Repeat behind.

28

Repeat behind.

29

Reverse-fold.
Repeat behind.

30

Reverse-fold.

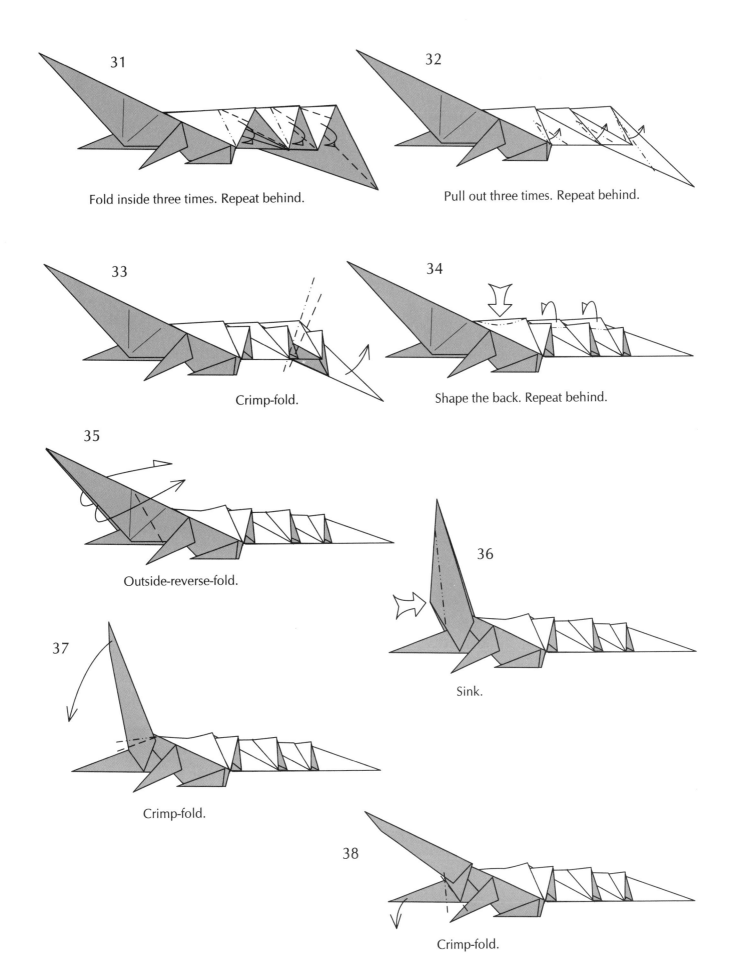

31

Fold inside three times. Repeat behind.

32

Pull out three times. Repeat behind.

33

Crimp-fold.

34

Shape the back. Repeat behind.

35

Outside-reverse-fold.

36

Sink.

37

Crimp-fold.

38

Crimp-fold.

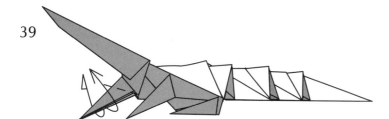

39

Outside-reverse-fold.

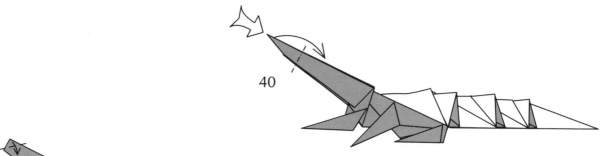

40

Fold inside.

41

Repeat behind.

42

Shape the head.

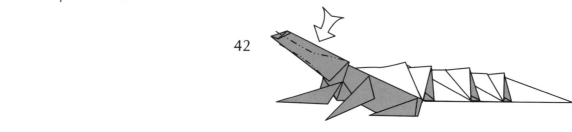

43

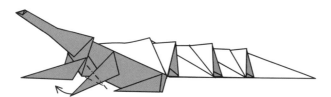

Crimp-fold. Repeat behind.

44

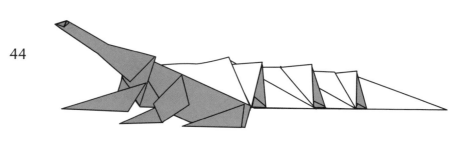

Crocodile

Smiling Frog

Designed by Roman Diaz
Uruguay

Originally diagrammed by
Roman Diaz

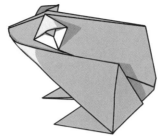

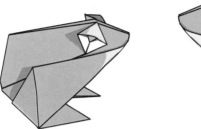

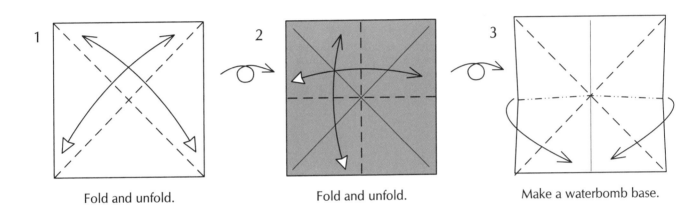

1 Fold and unfold.

2 Fold and unfold.

3 Make a waterbomb base.

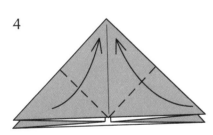

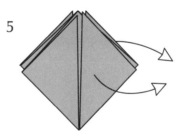

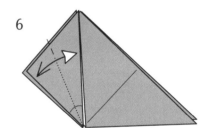

4 Repeat behind.

5 Unfold on one side.

6 Fold and unfold by the top. Repeat behind.

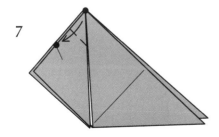

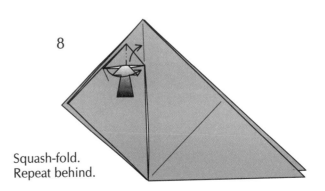

7 Repeat behind.

8 Squash-fold. Repeat behind.

9

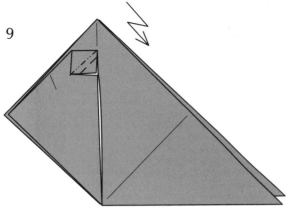

To form the eyes, spread the paper a little to do this fold comfortably. Repeat behind.

10

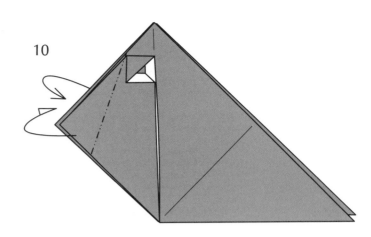

11

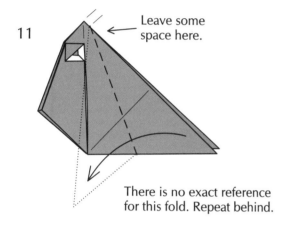

Leave some space here.

There is no exact reference for this fold. Repeat behind.

12

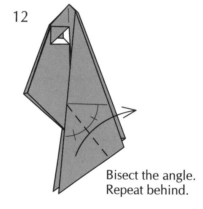

Bisect the angle. Repeat behind.

13

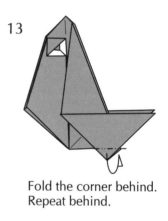

Fold the corner behind. Repeat behind.

14

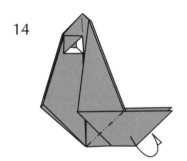

Repeat behind and rotate 90°.

15

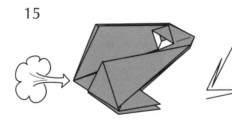

Inflate while keeping the two top edges together and spreading the legs.

16

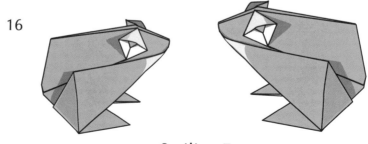

Smiling Frog

Reef Fish

Designed by Roman Diaz
Uruguay

Originally diagrammed by
Roman Diaz

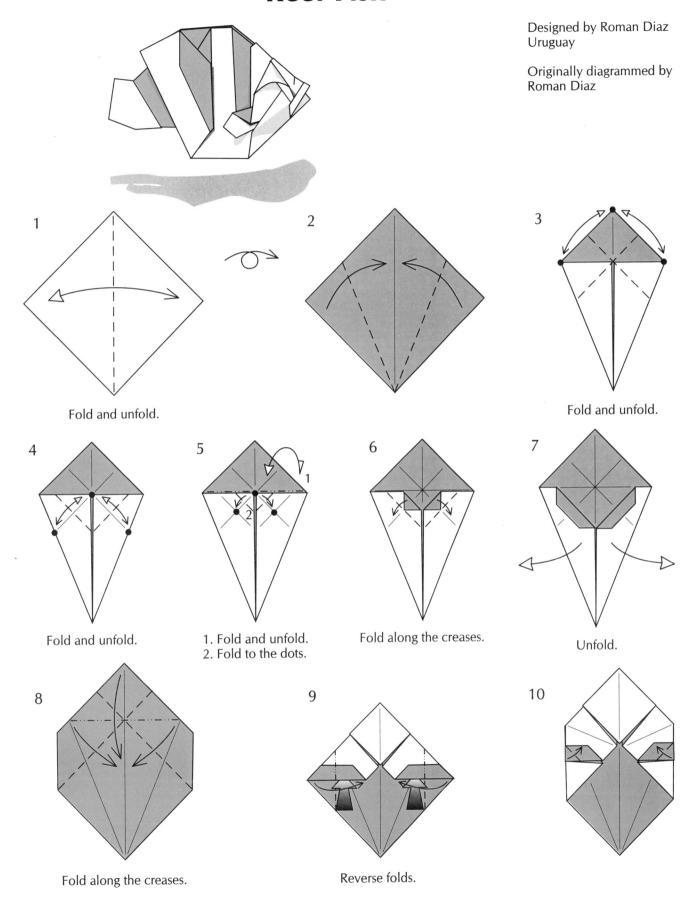

1

Fold and unfold.

2

3

Fold and unfold.

4

Fold and unfold.

5

1. Fold and unfold.
2. Fold to the dots.

6

Fold along the creases.

7

Unfold.

8

Fold along the creases.

9

Reverse folds.

10

11

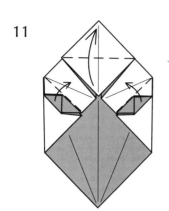

12

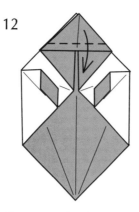

There is no landmark. Fold
all the layers together.

13

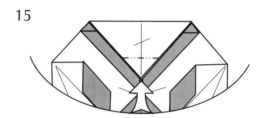

Fold and unfold by the diagonal.

14

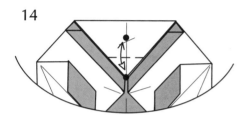

Fold and unfold the corner to
a little above the intersection.
There is no exact landmark.

15

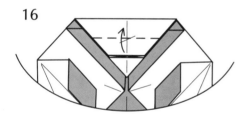

Open sink the point.

16

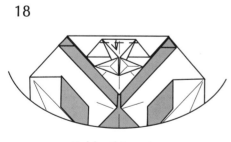

Spread the paper.

17

Spread-squash-fold.

18

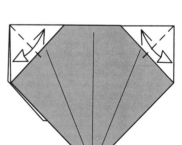

Fold a thin strip.

19

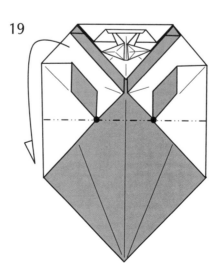

20

Fold and unfold
the top layers.

21

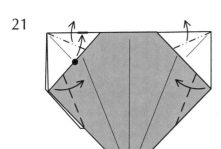

Bring the dot to the bold line.

22

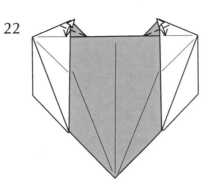

Fold and unfold.

23

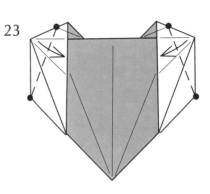

24

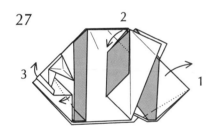

Squash folds.

25

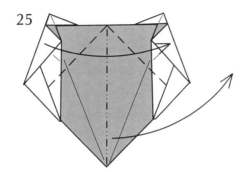

Close the model with a reverse fold for the tail.

26

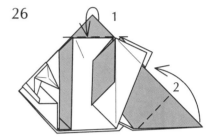

1. Tuck inside.
2. Outside-reverse-fold.

27

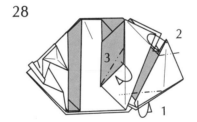

1. Slide the tail.
2. Fold the layers together.
3. Slide the upper lip to open the mouth a bit.
Repeat behind.

28

1. Repeat behind.
2. Reverse-fold.
3. Repeat behind.

29

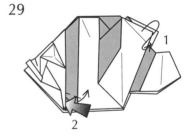

1. Lock the back by tucking the front half of the fin into the pocket of the other half.
2. Reverse-fold.

30

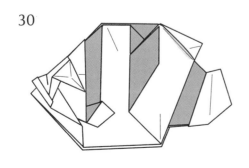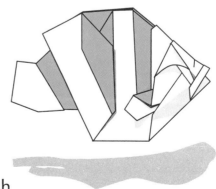

Reef Fish

Rooster

Designed by Gareth Louis
Australia

Originally diagrammed by
Gareth Louis

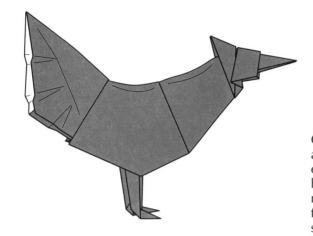

Gareth has been designing origami since a very young
age. His speciality include works of a novelty nature whilst
embedding elements of practicality. His Rooster is one of
his earliest works being originally designed in 1992 and
modified in 2005 to cater for the Chinese New Year
festivities. The Rooster incorporates a mechanical folding
sequence till the end where final shaping is required to
capture the realism of a Rooster.

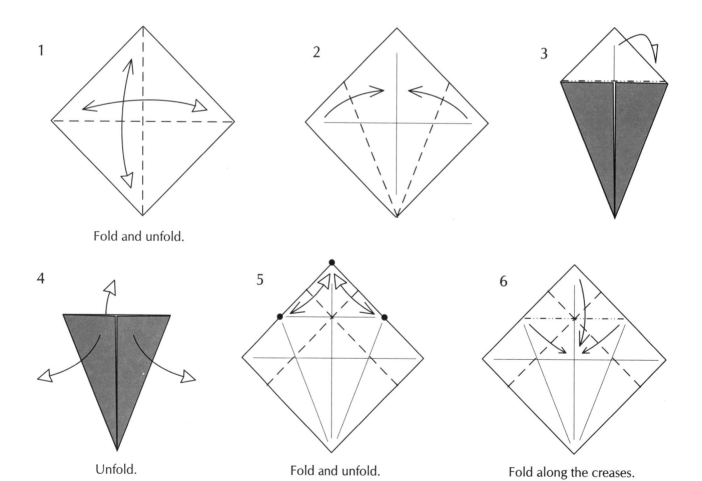

1 Fold and unfold.

2

3

4 Unfold.

5 Fold and unfold.

6 Fold along the creases.

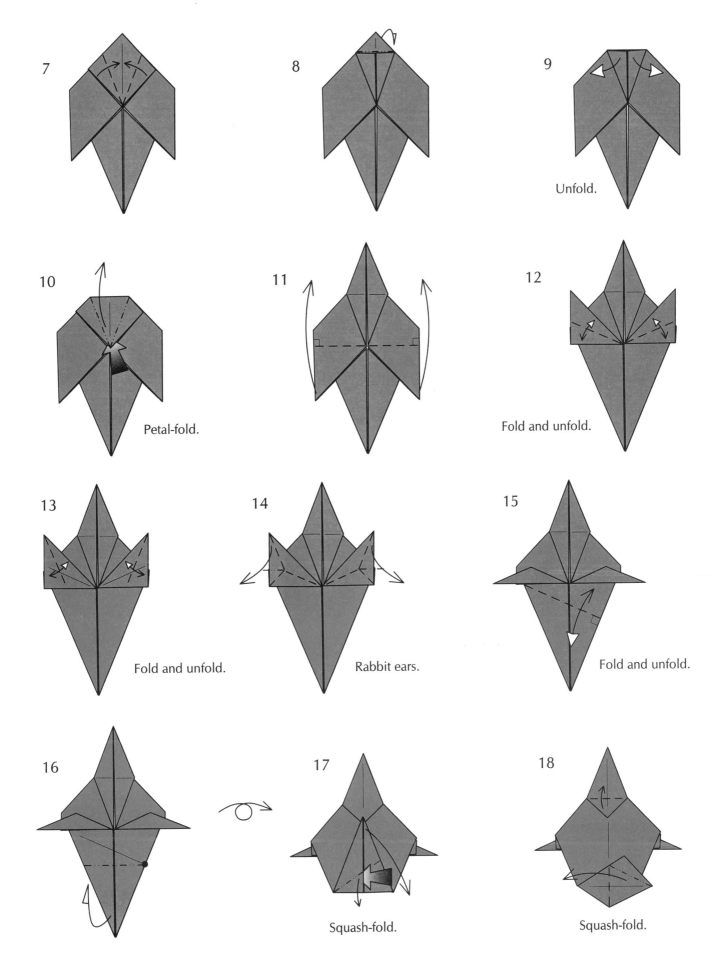

7

8

9

Unfold.

10

Petal-fold.

11

12

Fold and unfold.

13

Fold and unfold.

14

Rabbit ears.

15

Fold and unfold.

16

17

Squash-fold.

18

Squash-fold.

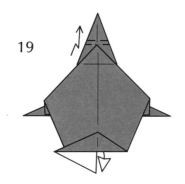

19

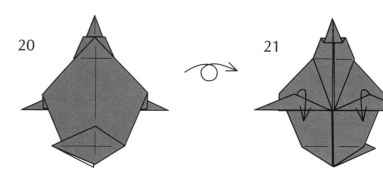

20

21

Pull out at the tail
and pleat the beak.

Swing the flaps down.

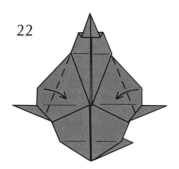

22

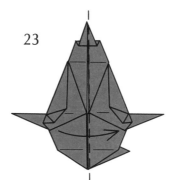

23

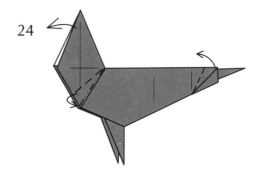

24

Crimp-fold the tail and
outside-reverse-fold the
crown.

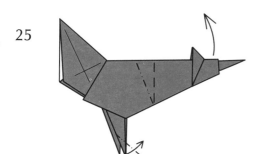

25

26

Valley-fold along the crease for the crimp
fold. Reverse-fold the foot and repeat behind.

Crimp-fold the head. Fold the layers
together at the leg. Repeat behind.

27

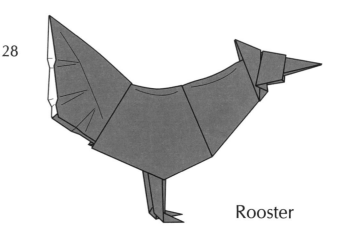

28

Pleat the plume and repeat
behind. Shape the back.

Rooter

Rooster

Kangaroo

Designed by Steven Casey
Australia

Originally diagrammed by
Steven Casey

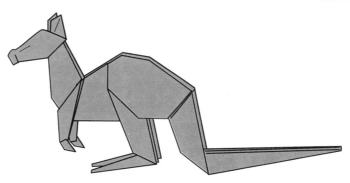

Steven became interested in Origami in 1970. His favourite style of origami is one piece, from a square, with no cutting. Steve enjoys creating origami with an Australian theme. This kangaroo was created in 1979. Steve is a sometime member of Melbourne Origami which came into existence in the late 90s. There is now a healthy interest in Origami in Melbourne due to the activities of the group.

1

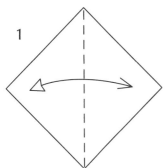

Fold and unfold.

2

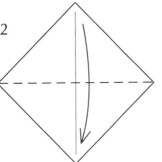

3

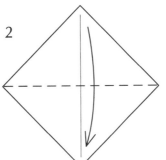

Fold and unfold
the top layer.

4

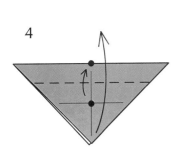

5

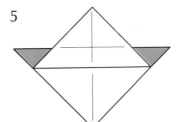

6

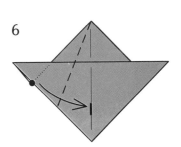

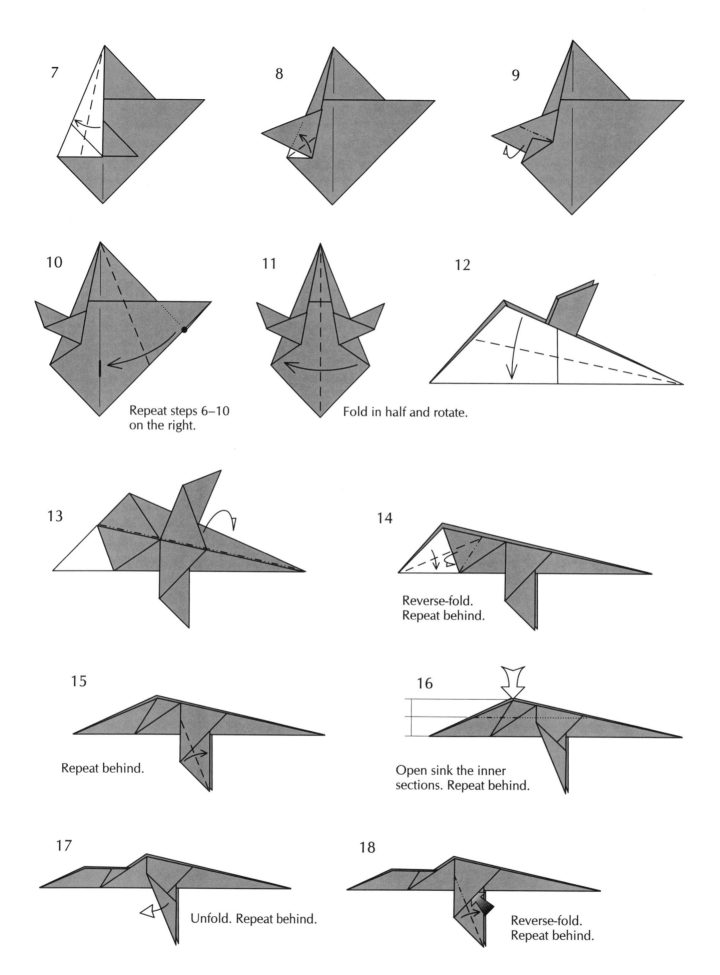

7

8

9

10

Repeat steps 6–10
on the right.

11

Fold in half and rotate.

12

13

14

Reverse-fold.
Repeat behind.

15

Repeat behind.

16

Open sink the inner
sections. Repeat behind.

17

Unfold. Repeat behind.

18

Reverse-fold.
Repeat behind.

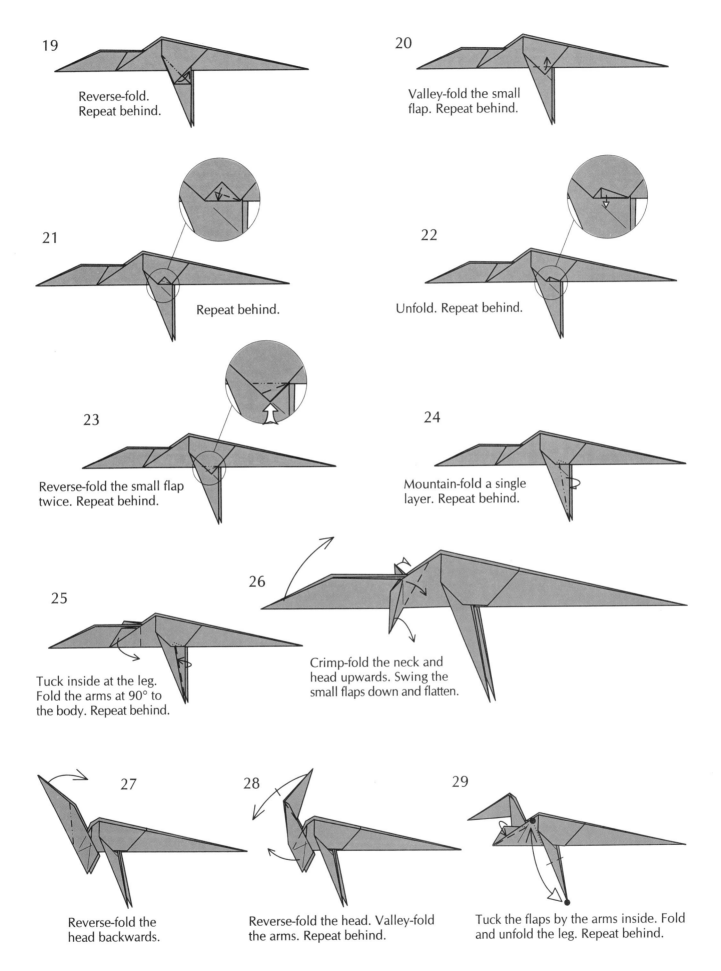

19
Reverse-fold.
Repeat behind.

20
Valley-fold the small
flap. Repeat behind.

21
Repeat behind.

22
Unfold. Repeat behind.

23
Reverse-fold the small flap
twice. Repeat behind.

24
Mountain-fold a single
layer. Repeat behind.

25
Tuck inside at the leg.
Fold the arms at 90° to
the body. Repeat behind.

26
Crimp-fold the neck and
head upwards. Swing the
small flaps down and flatten.

27
Reverse-fold the
head backwards.

28
Reverse-fold the head. Valley-fold
the arms. Repeat behind.

29
Tuck the flaps by the arms inside. Fold
and unfold the leg. Repeat behind.

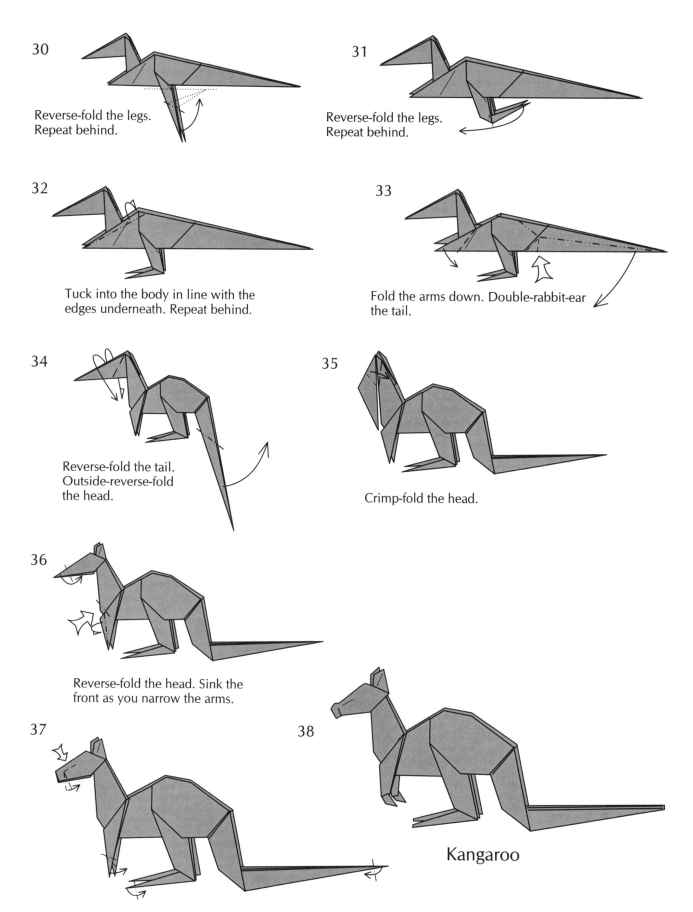

30 Reverse-fold the legs. Repeat behind.

31 Reverse-fold the legs. Repeat behind.

32 Tuck into the body in line with the edges underneath. Repeat behind.

33 Fold the arms down. Double-rabbit-ear the tail.

34 Reverse-fold the tail. Outside-reverse-fold the head.

35 Crimp-fold the head.

36 Reverse-fold the head. Sink the front as you narrow the arms.

37 Squash-fold the arms. Reverse-fold the tips of the hind legs and tail. Shape the head. Repeat behind.

38 Kangaroo

Coconut Tree

Designed by Quentin Trollip
South Africa

Originally diagrammed by
Quentin Trollip

Please visit www.liveorigami.com.

1

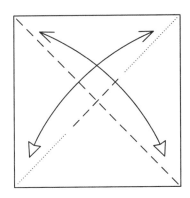

Fold and unfold. Make a
small crease in the center
in one direction.

2

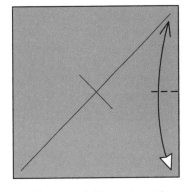

Fold and unfold on the right.

3

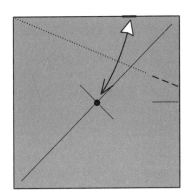

Fold and unfold on the right.

4

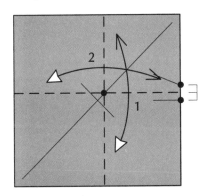

Fold and unfold so the dots on
the right meet. Repeat vertically.

5

Fold and unfold.

6

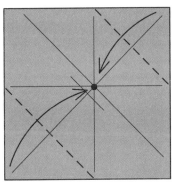

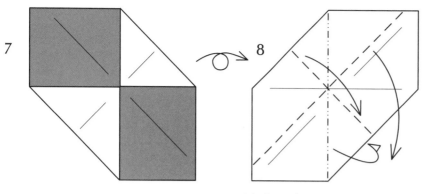

7

8

Fold along the creases. This is similar to folding the Waterbomb Base.

9

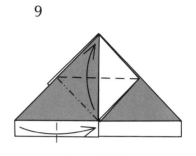

Squash-fold.

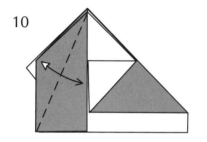

10

Fold and unfold.

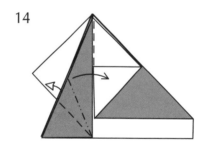

11

Fold and unfold.

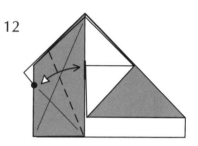

12

Fold and unfold.

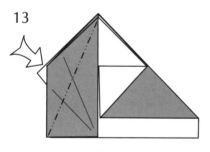

13

Sink.

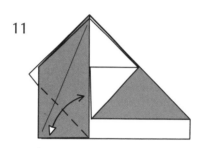

14

Fold one layer to the right and push some paper up from the inside.

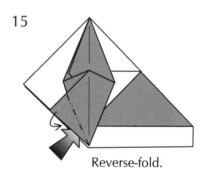

15

Reverse-fold.

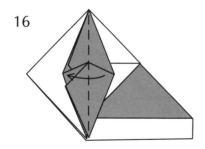

16

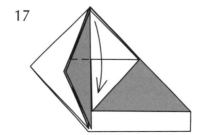

17

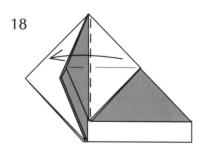

18

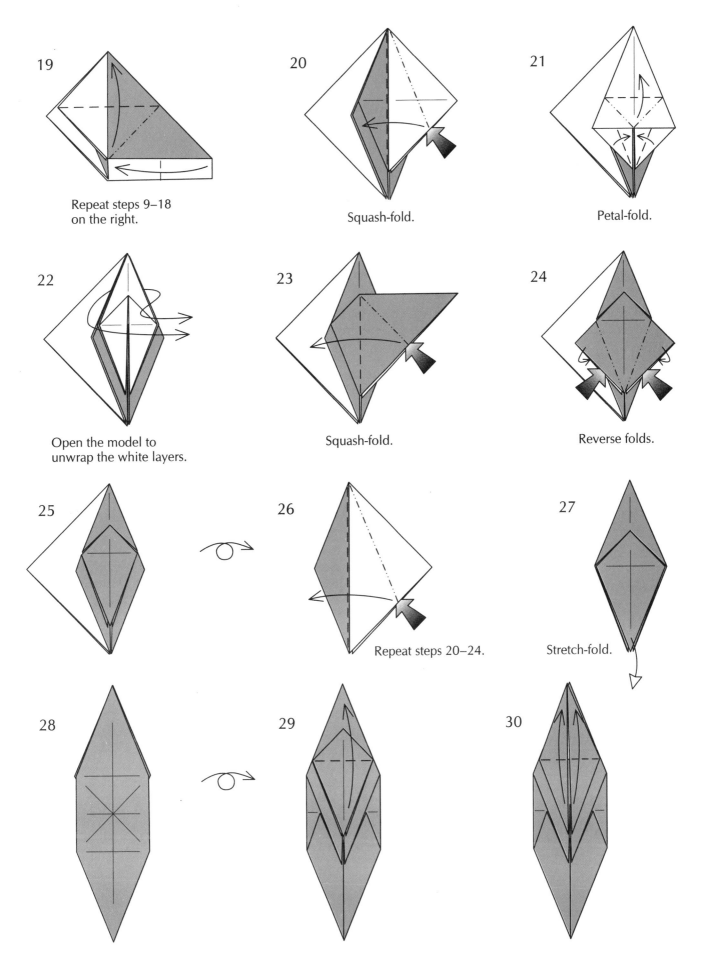

19
Repeat steps 9–18 on the right.

20
Squash-fold.

21
Petal-fold.

22
Open the model to unwrap the white layers.

23
Squash-fold.

24
Reverse folds.

25

26
Repeat steps 20–24.

27
Stretch-fold.

28

29

30

Coconut Tree 95

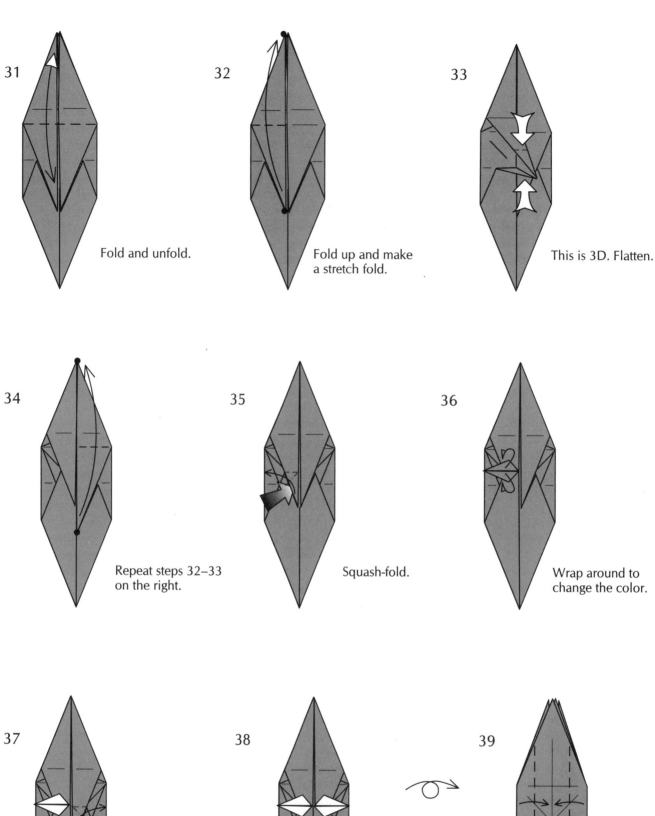

31   Fold and unfold.

32   Fold up and make a stretch fold.

33   This is 3D. Flatten.

34   Repeat steps 32–33 on the right.

35   Squash-fold.

36   Wrap around to change the color.

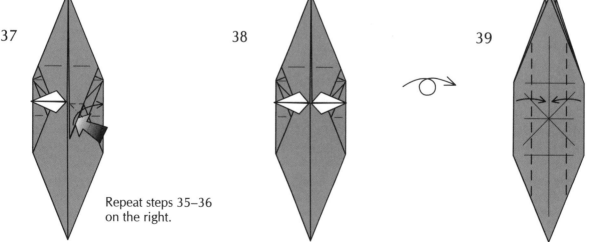

37   Repeat steps 35–36 on the right.

38

39

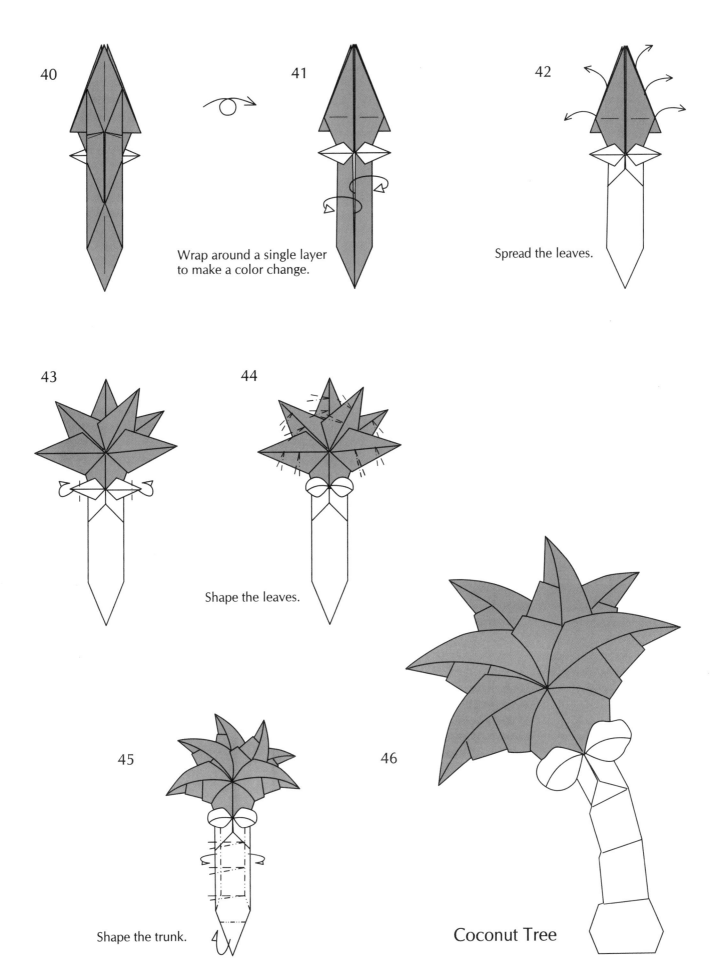

40

41

Wrap around a single layer
to make a color change.

42

Spread the leaves.

43

44

Shape the leaves.

45

Shape the trunk.

46

Coconut Tree

Polar Bear

Designed by Quentin Trollip
South Africa

Originally diagrammed by
Quentin Trollip

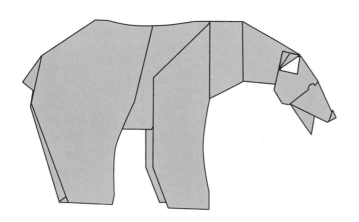

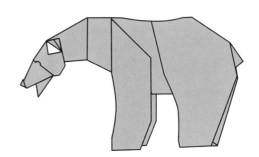

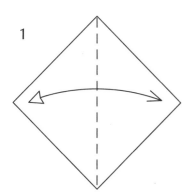

1

Fold and unfold.

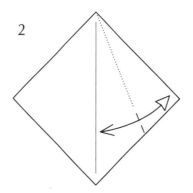

2

Fold and unfold at the edge.

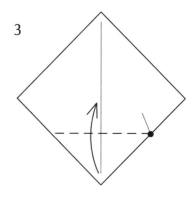

3

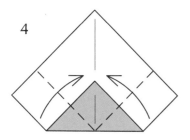

4

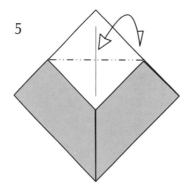

5

Fold and unfold.

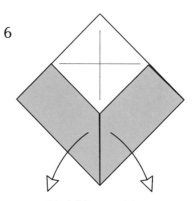

6

Unfold everything.

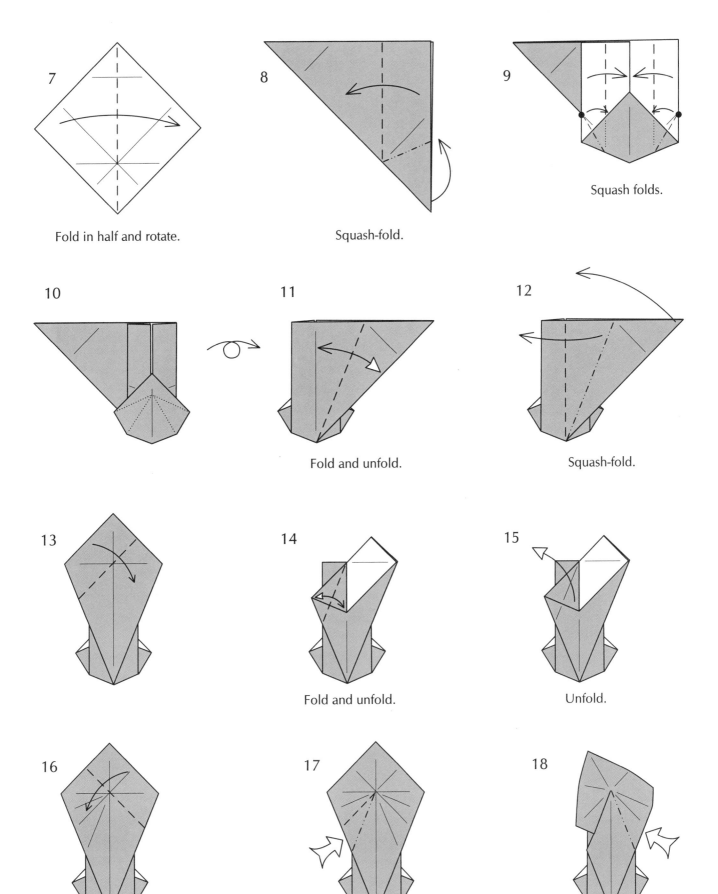

7 Fold in half and rotate.

8 Squash-fold.

9 Squash folds.

10

11 Fold and unfold.

12 Squash-fold.

13

14 Fold and unfold.

15 Unfold.

16 Repeat steps 13–15 on the right.

17 Reverse-fold in and out. The model will not lie flat.

18 Reverse-fold and flatten.

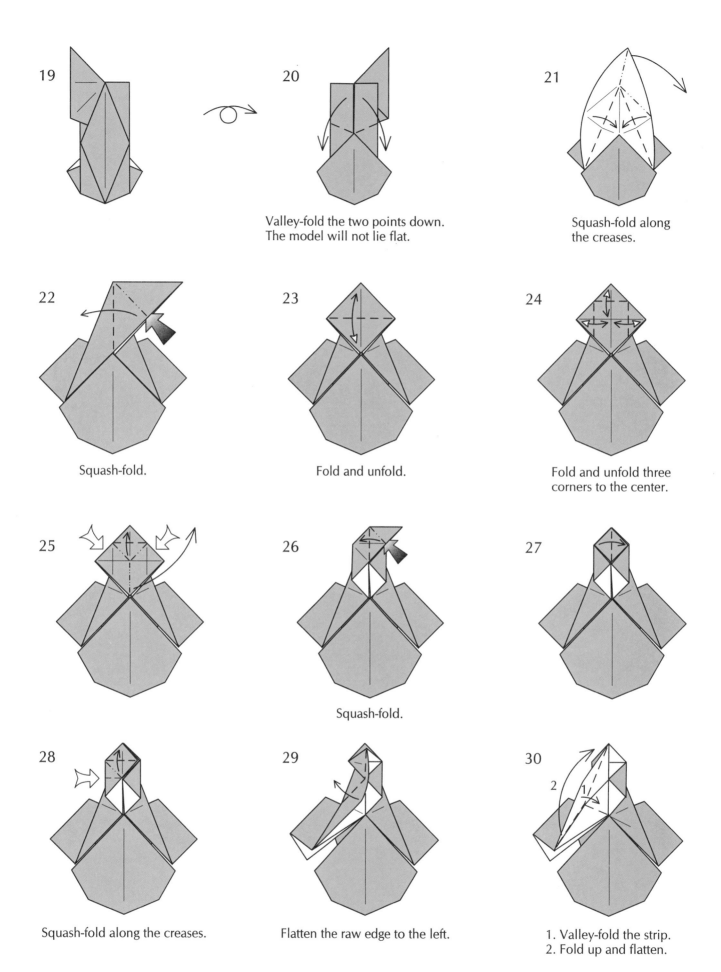

19

20

Valley-fold the two points down.
The model will not lie flat.

21

Squash-fold along
the creases.

22

Squash-fold.

23

Fold and unfold.

24

Fold and unfold three
corners to the center.

25

26

Squash-fold.

27

28

Squash-fold along the creases.

29

Flatten the raw edge to the left.

30

1. Valley-fold the strip.
2. Fold up and flatten.

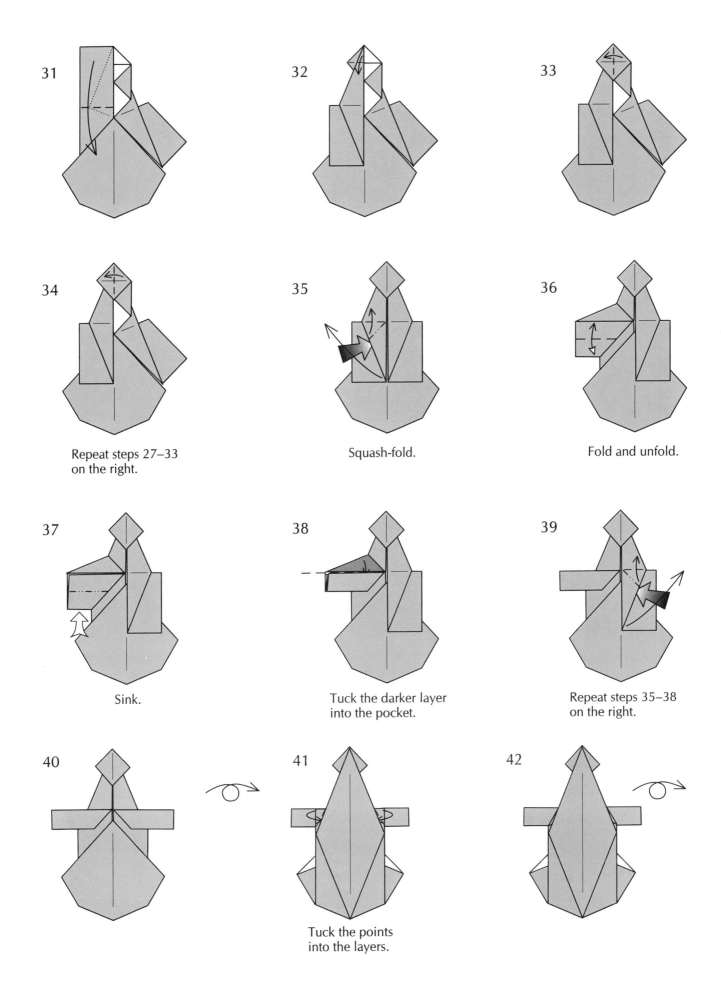

31

32

33

34

Repeat steps 27–33
on the right.

35

Squash-fold.

36

Fold and unfold.

37

Sink.

38

Tuck the darker layer
into the pocket.

39

Repeat steps 35–38
on the right.

40

41

Tuck the points
into the layers.

42

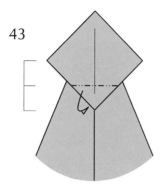

43

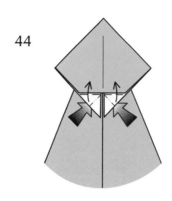

44

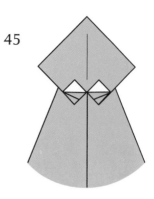

45

Head detail.

Squash folds.

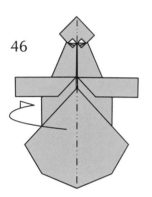

46

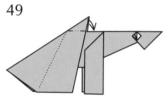

47

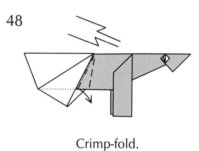

48

Fold in half and rotate.

The darker layer is cut from the next diagram.

Crimp-fold.

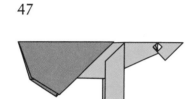

49

50

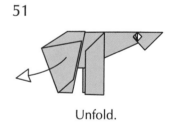

51

Tuck inside with a reverse fold.

Bring the edges together.

Unfold.

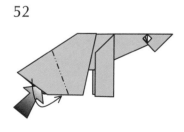

52

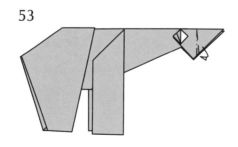

53

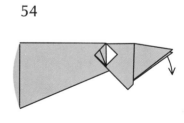

54

Reverse-fold.

Make a small crimp fold.

Pull the lower jaw down.

55

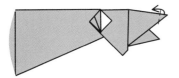

Outside-reverse-fold
the tip of the nose.

56

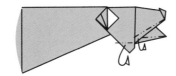

Shape the head. Repeat behind.

57

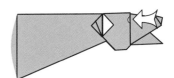

Shape the eyes.

58

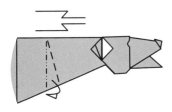

Crimp-fold.

59

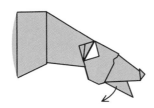

Rotate the head down.

60

Crimp-fold the tail.

61

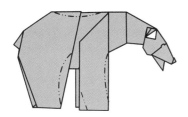

Shape the body and make it 3D.

62

Polar Bear

Ganesha

Designed by Kamlesh Gandhi
India

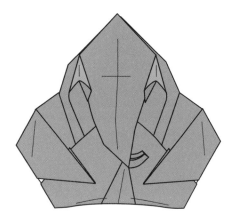

Email: kamleshgandhi87@hotmail.com

Website of Origami Mitra in India:
www.origami-mitra.com

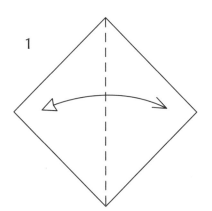

1

Fold and unfold.

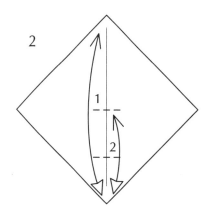

2

Fold and unfold in half twice.

3

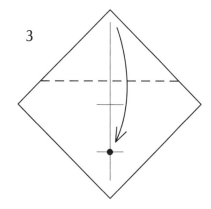

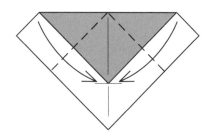

4

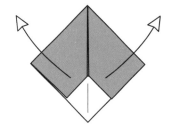

5

Unfold.

6

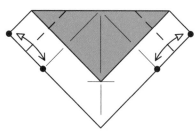

Fold and unfold.

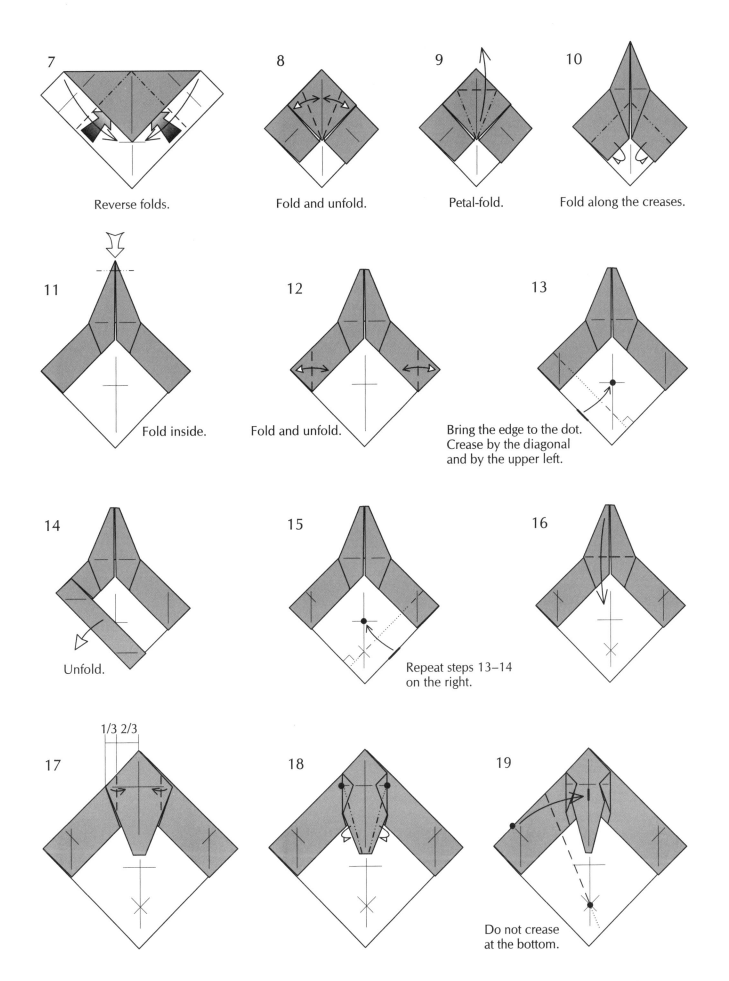

7 Reverse folds.

8 Fold and unfold.

9 Petal-fold.

10 Fold along the creases.

11 Fold inside.

12 Fold and unfold.

13 Bring the edge to the dot. Crease by the diagonal and by the upper left.

14 Unfold.

15 Repeat steps 13–14 on the right.

16

17 1/3 2/3

18

19 Do not crease at the bottom.

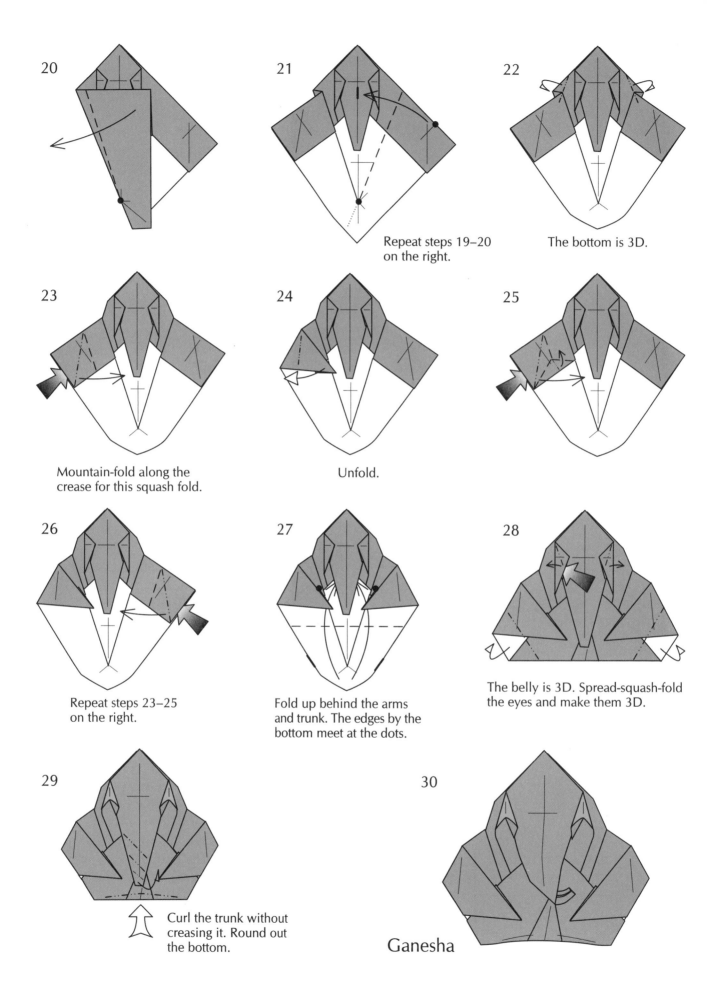

20

21 Repeat steps 19–20 on the right.

22 The bottom is 3D.

23 Mountain-fold along the crease for this squash fold.

24 Unfold.

25

26 Repeat steps 23–25 on the right.

27 Fold up behind the arms and trunk. The edges by the bottom meet at the dots.

28 The belly is 3D. Spread-squash-fold the eyes and make them 3D.

29 Curl the trunk without creasing it. Round out the bottom.

30 Ganesha

Boat

Designed by Kuldip Thatte
India

Originally diagrammed by
Kuldip Thatte

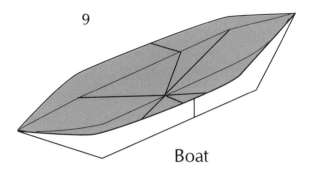

9

Boat

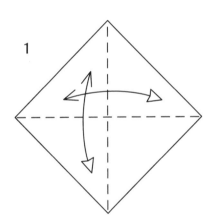

1

Fold and unfold
along the diagonals

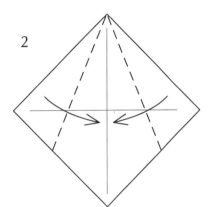

2

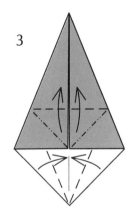

3

Squash folds.

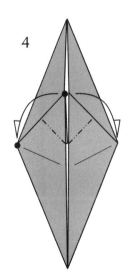

4

Fold behind.

5

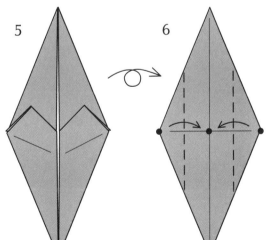

6

7

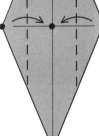

8

Wrap around.

Open.

Fox

Designed by Fumiaki Kawahata
Japan

Originally diagrammed by
Fumiaki Kawahata

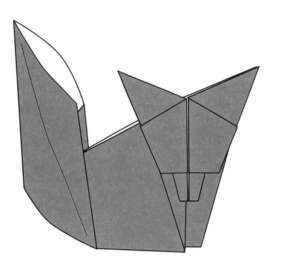

1

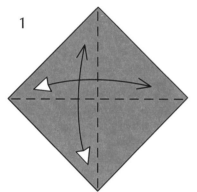

Fold and unfold.

2

Fold to the top.

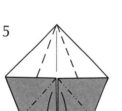

3

4

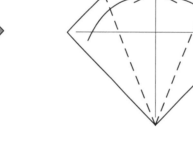

Squash folds.

5

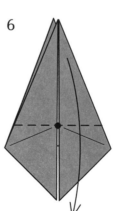

Fold the top layer down.

6

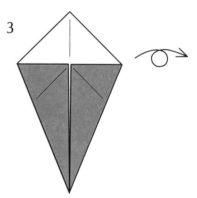

7

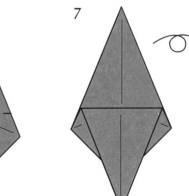

8

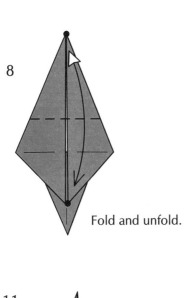

Fold and unfold.

9

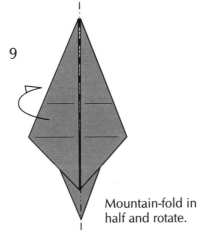

Mountain-fold in half and rotate.

10

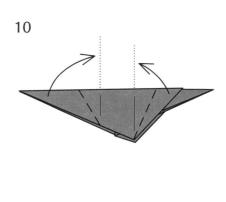

11

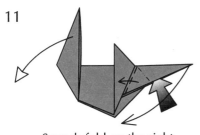

Squash-fold on the right and unfold on the left.

12

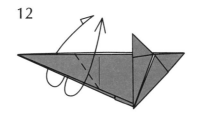

Outside-reverse-fold.

13

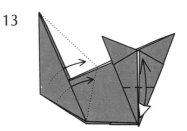

On left pull out from inside. Fold and unfold on right.

14

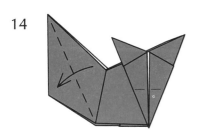

15

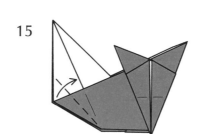

16

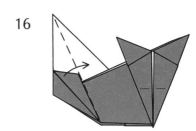

17

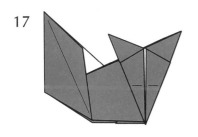

Repeat steps 13–16 behind.

18

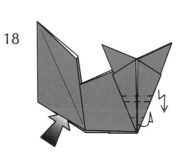

Make the tail 3D.

19

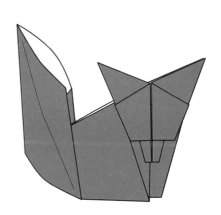

Fox

Pig

Designed by Nguyen Hung Cuong
Vietnam

Originally diagrammed by
Nguyen Hung Cuong

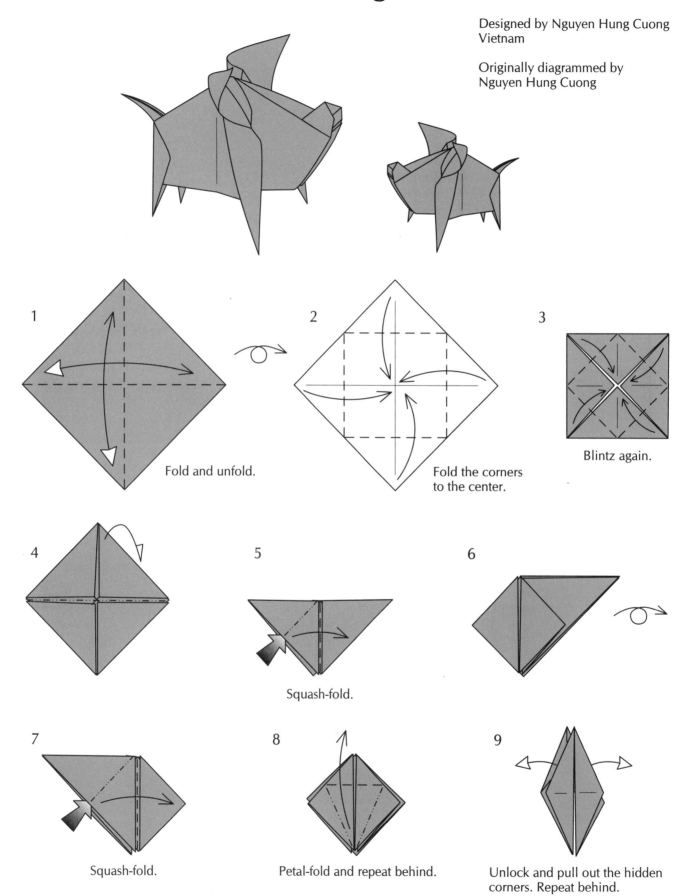

1

Fold and unfold.

2

Fold the corners
to the center.

3

Blintz again.

4

5

Squash-fold.

6

7

Squash-fold.

8

Petal-fold and repeat behind.

9

Unlock and pull out the hidden
corners. Repeat behind.

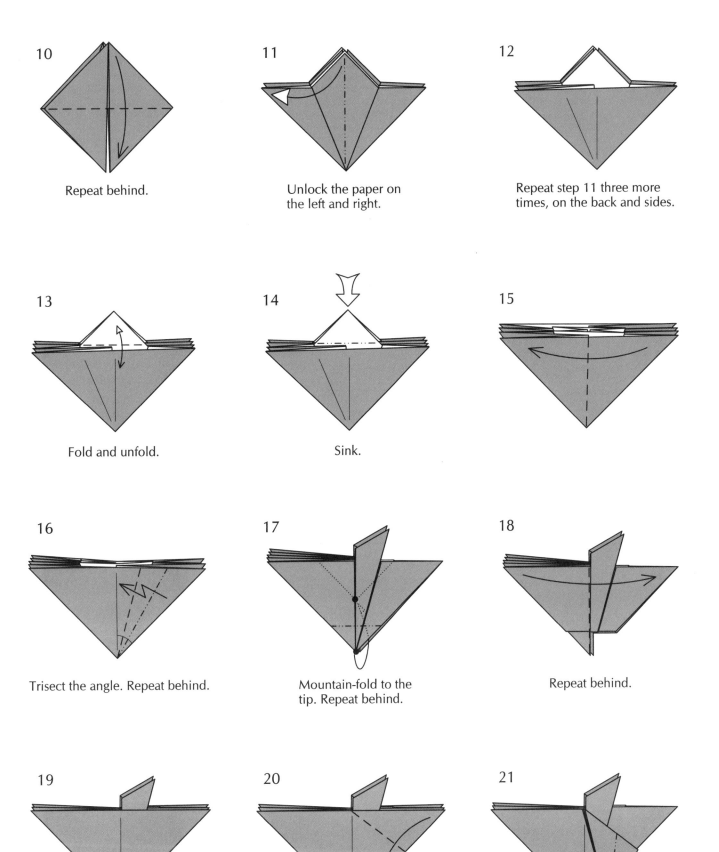

10

Repeat behind.

11

Unlock the paper on
the left and right.

12

Repeat step 11 three more
times, on the back and sides.

13

Fold and unfold.

14

Sink.

15

16

Trisect the angle. Repeat behind.

17

Mountain-fold to the
tip. Repeat behind.

18

Repeat behind.

19

Repeat behind.

20

Repeat behind.

21

Repeat behind.

22

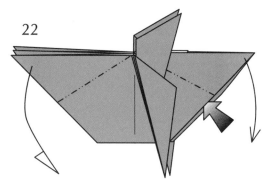

Reverse-fold at the head.
Repeat behind at the leg.

23

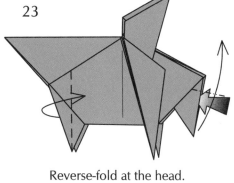

Reverse-fold at the head.
Repeat behind at the leg.

24

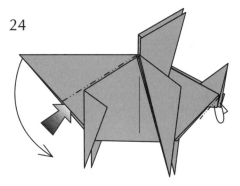

Repeat behind at the head.
Reverse-fold at the tail.

25

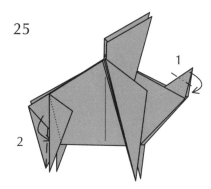

1. Reverse-fold at the head.
2. Reverse-fold. Mountain-fold
along the dotted (hidden) line
and repeat behind at the tail.

26

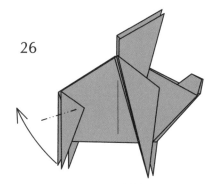

Reverse-fold.

27

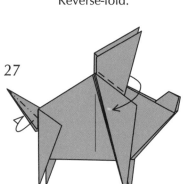

Open the ear and thin
the tail. Repeat behind.

28

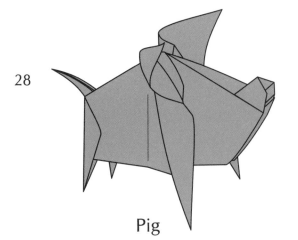

Pig

Fiery Dragon

Designed by Chan Pak Hei , Kade
China

Originally diagramed by
Chan Hon Fai , Jacky

Website: http://tw.myblog.yahoo.com/kade-x
email: kade@live.hk

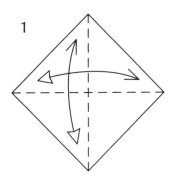

1

Fold and unfold.

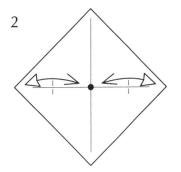

2

Fold two corners to
the center and unfold.

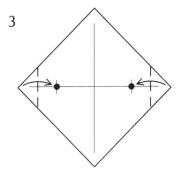

3

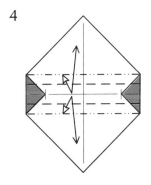

4

Fold and unfold.

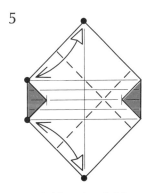

5

Fold and unfold.

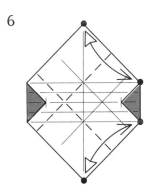

6

Fold and unfold.

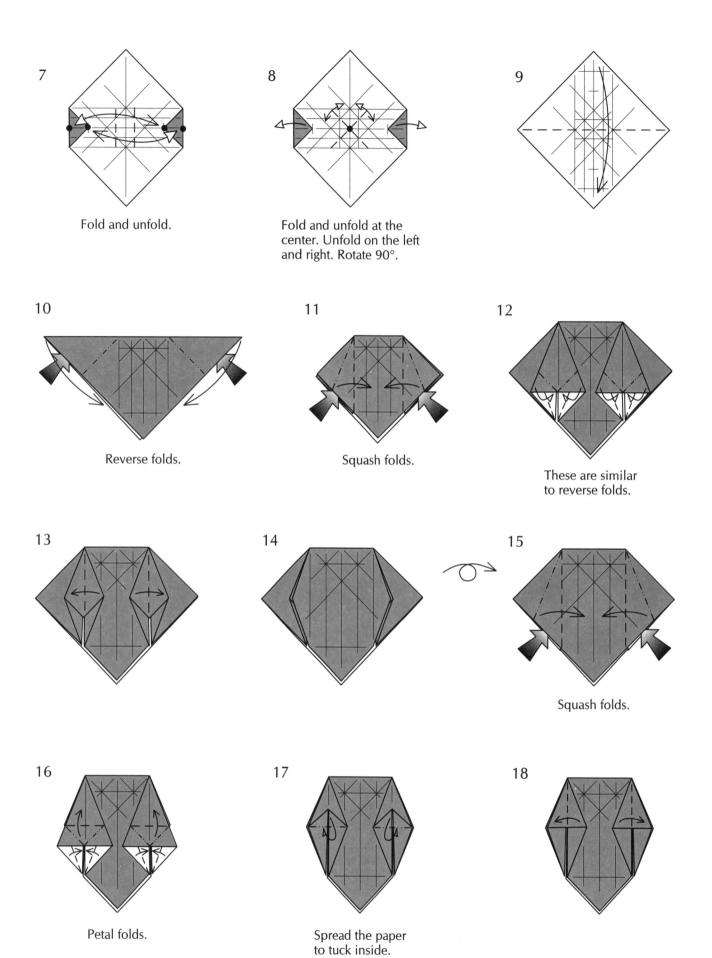

7

Fold and unfold.

8

Fold and unfold at the center. Unfold on the left and right. Rotate 90°.

9

10

Reverse folds.

11

Squash folds.

12

These are similar to reverse folds.

13

14

15

Squash folds.

16

Petal folds.

17

Spread the paper to tuck inside.

18

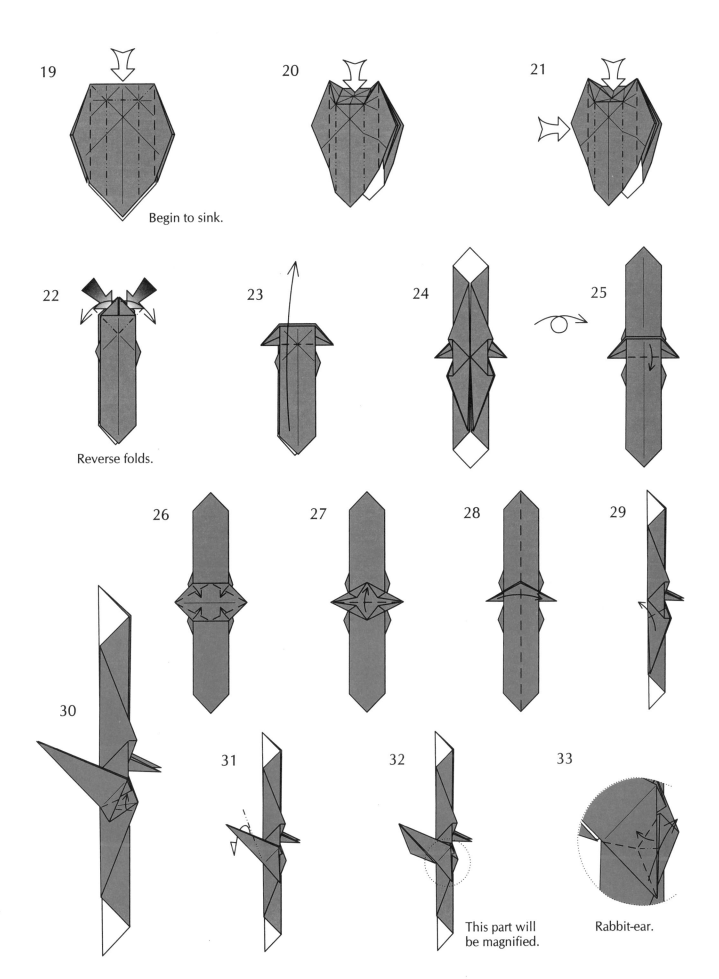

19

20

21

Begin to sink.

22

Reverse folds.

23

24

25

26

27

28

29

30

31

32

This part will be magnified.

33

Rabbit-ear.

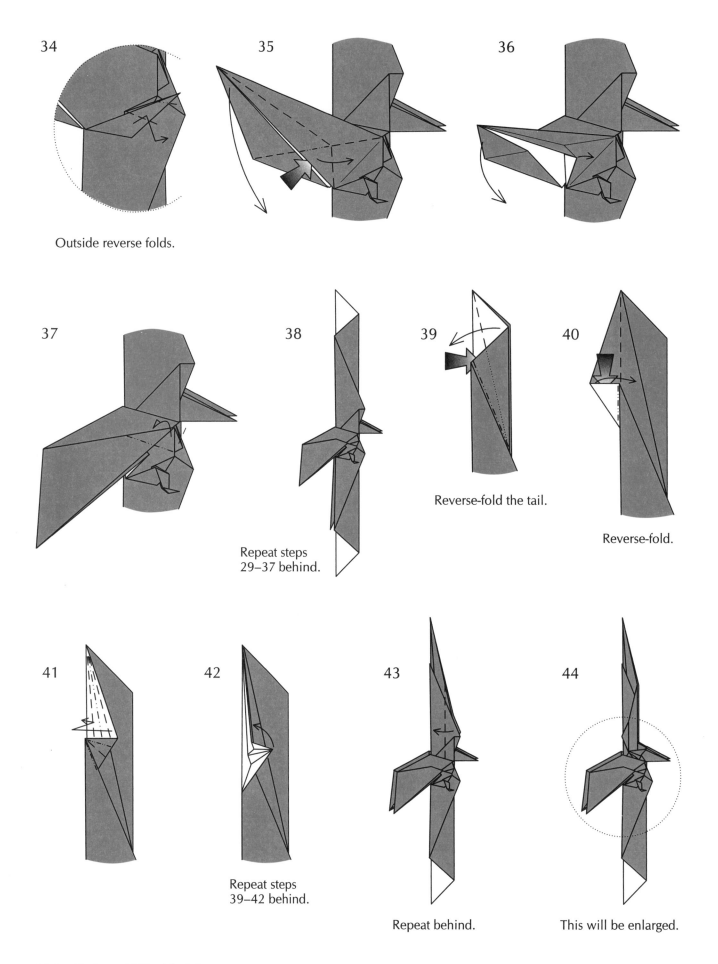

34

Outside reverse folds.

35

36

37

38

Repeat steps
29–37 behind.

39

Reverse-fold the tail.

40

Reverse-fold.

41

42

Repeat steps
39–42 behind.

43

Repeat behind.

44

This will be enlarged.

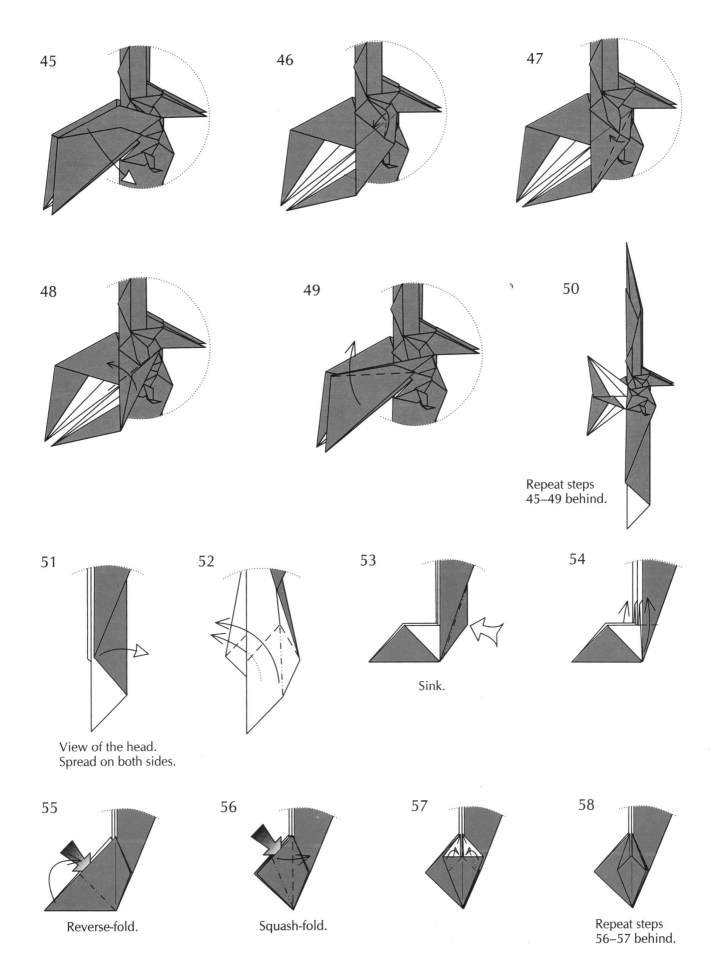

45

46

47

48

49

50

Repeat steps
45–49 behind.

51

View of the head.
Spread on both sides.

52

53

Sink.

54

55

Reverse-fold.

56

Squash-fold.

57

58

Repeat steps
56–57 behind.

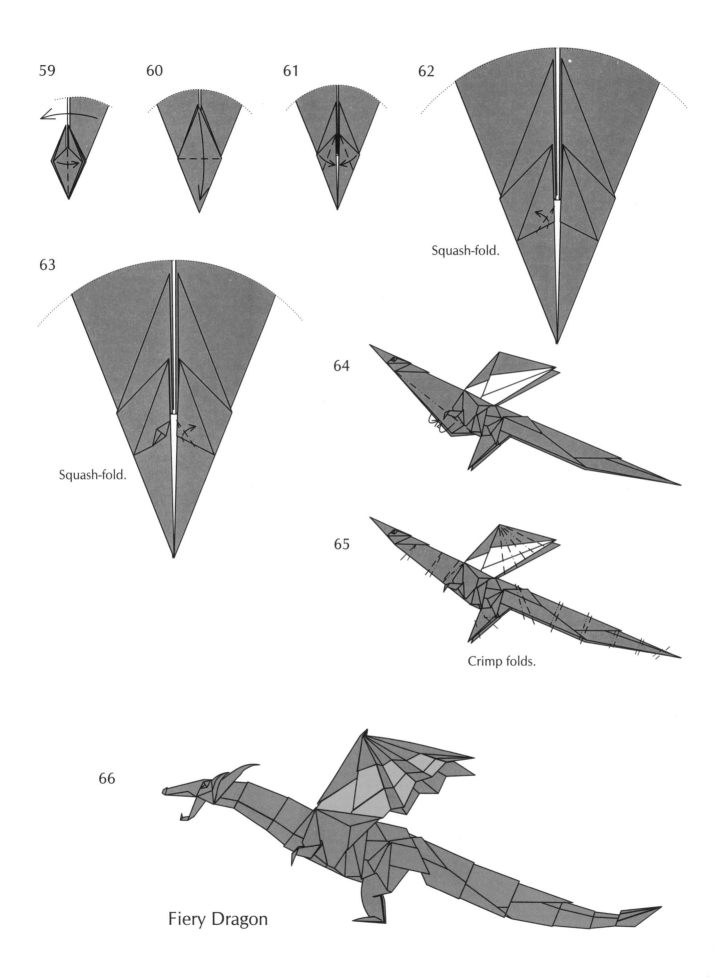

59

60

61

62

Squash-fold.

63

Squash-fold.

64

65

Crimp folds.

66

Fiery Dragon

Basic Folds

Rabbit Ear.

To fold a rabbit ear, one corner is
folded in half and laid down to a side.

1

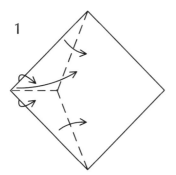

Fold a rabbit ear.

2

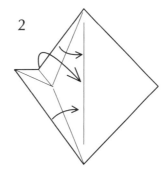

A 3D intermediate step.

3

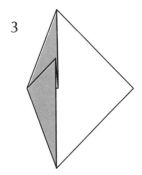

Squash Fold.

In a squash fold, some paper is opened
and then made flat. The shaded arrow
shows where to place your finger.

1

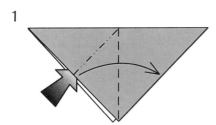

Squash-fold.

2

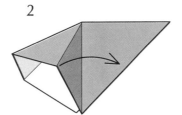

A 3D intermediate step.

3

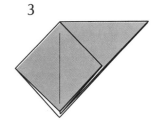

Petal Fold.

In a petal fold, one point is folded up while
two opposite sides meet each other.

1

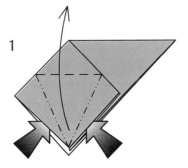

Petal-fold.

2

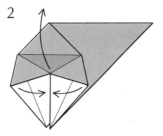

A 3D intermediate step.

3

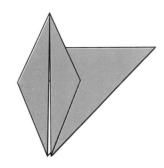

Inside Reverse Fold.

In an inside reverse fold, some paper is folded between layers. Here are two examples.

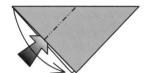

Reverse-fold.

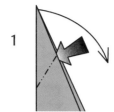
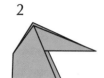

Reverse-fold.

Outside Reverse Fold.

Much of the paper must be unfolded to make an outside reverse fold.

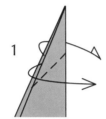

Outside-reverse-fold.

Crimp Fold.

A crimp fold is a combination of two reverse folds.

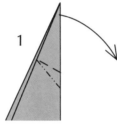

Crimp-fold.

Sink Fold.

In a sink fold, some of the paper without edges is folded inside. To do this fold, much of the model must be unfolded.

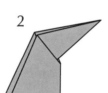

Sink.

Spread Squash Fold.

A cross between a squash fold and sink fold, some paper in the center is spread apart and then made flat.

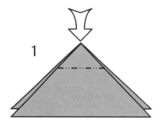

Spread-squash-fold.

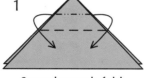
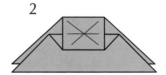